Les and Ernest, 1923

The Hemingway children (Ernest holding Les on right)

20 CENTES

100 CENT

NEW ATL

CENTE

NEW ATLAN

ES * POSTAGE

100 CENTES

honouring
LYNDON
BAINES
JOHNSON
protector
of the
entire

I0953396

and V

ip them against the shi
country above the high-ti
"Since you can't claim isla
ause they're all owned by
told me, "I decided to buil
and this rock just below th
w I've got the smallest cou
rld, the 22nd republic in t
emisphere."

* * *

So far, Leicester has sp   he got
30,000 on his project, most of w   "My
from the brisk sale of his 1962 book,
Brother, Ernest Hemingway." And he ex-
pects many thousands more.

"But," he said, cannily, "I'm going to
profit in many ways. I'll make money and
I'll be absolutely, completely independent
as will other citizens of New Atlantis
We're going to be an example for othe
people who long for absolute freedor
We'll be a counterpart to the deadly seriou
ness of life in a rut."

The money, Leicester figures, will con
from the sale of New Atlantis stamps a
coins (what collector would want to
without a batch of stamps and coins fr
the smallest country in the world!), fro
and from the newspaper he's
New Atlantis.

The Blue Stream off Cuba

trustwor
tunities for success in
entire

JOHNSON
protector

HUNTING
WITH
HEMINGWAY

Leicester Hemingway, 1918

RIVERHEAD BOOKS

New York

2000

HUNTING

WITH

HEMINGWAY

Based on the Stories of
Leicester Hemingway

HILARY HEMINGWAY
AND
JEFFRY P. LINDSAY

Some names have been changed to protect
the privacy of certain individuals.

Riverhead Books
a member of
Penguin Putnam Inc.
375 Hudson Street
New York, NY 10014

Photographs in this book are from *My Brother, Ernest Hemingway,*
© copyright 1996 by Doris Hemingway,
and are used by permission of Pineapple Press, Inc.

Library of Congress Cataloging-in-Publication Data

Hemingway, Hilary.
Hunting with Hemingway : based on the stories of Leicester Hemingway /
Hilary Hemingway and Jeffry P. Lindsay.
p.   cm.
ISBN 1-57322-159-7
1. Hemingway, Ernest, 1899–1961.   2. Hemingway, Leicester, 1915–1982—Family.
3. Authors, American—20th century—Biography.   4. Journalists—
United States—Biography.   5. Brothers—United States—Biography.
6. Hunters—United States—Biography.   7. Hunting.   I. Lindsay, Jeffry P.   II. Title.
PS3515.E37 Z6172   2000   00-036994
813'.52—dc21
[B]

Printed in the United States of America
1   3   5   7   9   10   8   6   4   2

This book is printed on acid-free paper. ∞

BOOK DESIGN BY AMANDA DEWEY

FOR OUR DAUGHTERS,

T. L. BEAR

AND POOKIE

Acknowledgments

This book could not have been written without the kind support, enthusiasm, and severe nudging from friends and family members. We would like to thank Carlene Brennen, Annie Hemingway-Feuer, Bill Feuer, Dr. August and Tommie Freundlich, Ed Gorman, Jake and Mary Hemingway, Peter and Natalie Hemingway, Patrick and Carol Hemingway, Dr. Jim Nagle, George Nixon, Jack Smith, Julius Szalay, Trish and Rob MacGregor, James Lee Burke, and Randy Wayne White; Jimmy Vines of the Vines Literary Agency for his creative insight; and Erin Bush and our fabulous editor, Lady Celina Spiegel, at Riverhead Books.

And of course, Doris and Les Hemingway.

Hunting

with

Hemingway

Truth is a strange thing, kid.

—LEICESTER HEMINGWAY

Author's Note

The story of this book begins on January 17, 1997, the day my mother, Doris Hemingway, died, when I received from her a tape of my father, Leicester Hemingway, telling stories of hunting with his brother Ernest. Later my husband, Jeff, and I found corresponding manuscript pages and integrated these written stories with the much shorter tales on the tape. *Hunting with Hemingway* is in my voice, but it is not my work alone. Though Jeff and I have each had successful solo writing careers, in the last decade we've shared the responsibilities of book writing, marriage, and raising our daughters as a great collaborative work—equal in effort, emotion, and thought. Jeff listened to the tape with me and shared my rediscovery of my father.

This collection of his hunting adventures with Papa taught me about my father's courage, sense of humor, genuine compassion, and the Hemingway respect for death without suffering. In putting this book together, I was finally able to mourn my father. In his stories, I rediscovered his love of life.

It is a Hemingway trait to embellish one's own accomplishments. My father did this for both his own amusement and the amusement of others. It is my hope that the adventure stories in this book will be enjoyed in the spirit of playfulness in which we believe they were intended. I'm pleased to share with you what Jeff and I learned about two unique Hemingway brothers and their highly unusual hunting adventures.

—Hilary Hemingway

FOR A QUARTER of a century, Ernest Hemingway's last unpublished book, a fictionalized account of his 1953 safari to Africa, sat sealed in two libraries. It was read only by my relatives, some publishers, and a few scholars.

July 21, 1999, celebrated not just Ernest Hemingway's hundredth birthday but also the publication of *True at First Light*. The manuscript contains more comedy than Papa's usual works. The story describes big-cat hunts, a tribal uprising, and Papa's efforts to live among the Wakamba people of East Africa. There is also a maybe-true, maybe-not, account of Papa's marriage to an eighteen-year-old African woman.

My cousin Patrick Hemingway, Ernest's middle son and the editor of the manuscript, believed that the lingering element of ambiguity would have been important to Papa. Ernest adored a good joke as much as a good story. In this he was not alone. My father, Ernest's brother, also enjoyed telling a good story, and had a true gift for it.

Now, while most men might think growing up as the kid brother of Ernest Hemingway would be ideal, there were times—when Papa tested the strength, courage, and marksmanship of those around him—when being that close could be uncomfortable. My dad never talked about these things, at least not to me.

But then, in 1997, I made a discovery that led to the writing of this book. I offer it as a tribute to both brothers, both hunters and enthusiasts of tall tales.

IT STARTED ON JANUARY 17, 1997, the day my mother died. She had lost her long battle with lung cancer and found peace in death. No more chemo, radiation, morphine, oxygen tubes. Mom was free.

But after six years of caring for her, I was a wreck. A week after Mom's passing, my brothers joined my sister and me at our house in southwest Florida. We sat down together to go through Mom's will. Together, we opened her safe-deposit box, where we found insurance and house papers—and four manila envelopes. My sister Anne opened the one with her name on it. We saw that she had been given a few of my mother's rings. My brothers, Jake and Peter, had been left some of our father's coin collection.

Inside my envelope was an old audiocassette. It was labeled "Les Hemingway" in block print. I didn't recognize the handwriting, and I had no idea why Mom had given me an old tape of Dad's. Was this some final message from my father? Although he had died almost fifteen years earlier, I thought of him often. I missed him as I now missed my mother. If I sat quietly, I could hear their laughter or the calm of their voices. I shook the tape like a box of Good & Plenty candy. What was it?

"Aren't you going to play it, Hil?" my sister asked as I sat in the big old rocking chair in our living room.

"Sure, when I find a cassette machine. I think all we have is a CD player."

I put the cassette aside and spent most of the day sorting through the estate's papers, too occupied with red tape and worn down by sadness to think about my strange inheritance.

Later that day I needed a break and wandered through the house. Hope Hospice workers had come and cleared away Mom's medical bed and assorted bottles and equipment. My sister had taken a load of Mom's clothing over to the Kiwanis thrift store. With all of her stuff gone, Mom's death really started to seem final. There was an unsettling echo in her deserted rooms. And while my Mom had lived on one side of the house, without her every room seemed empty.

Next to my husband, Mom was my best friend. I paused in the dining room to straighten a wedding picture. There she was—arms around Jeff and me. The only advice she had ever given me was never to marry a writer and never to become one. Of course, that's what I had done, just as she had. And when she became sick, I knew I had to come home.

Jeff and I left California, where we had a writing deal pending with Warner Brothers. Our plan was to care for Mom for the six months the doctors had given her. But six years later, Mom was living proof that writers can rewrite their own endings.

We bought a larger house together over on Florida's west coast. And for the most part, Mom seemed happy. Jeff and I began new careers writing novels and had just signed a three-book deal when Mom let go. I didn't blame her; she had grown tired of the pain, the morphine, handfuls of pills, the constant nebulizer treatments, the full-time oxygen, the living in a bed and a wheelchair.

I couldn't blame her—but I missed her. I felt the tears welling up again. I turned away from the pictures and went to find comfort in the nursery with our baby daughter, a curly-headed blond cherub. She was still asleep. God had taken Mom with one hand and had given me an angel with the other.

We called our baby Pookie. For privacy's sake, we'll leave it at that. But it's also a tradition in my family and my husband's to give nicknames. I grew up as Hillsides, my dad was the Baron, and Ernest was known as Papa. My husband, Jeff, has been called Flash most of his life. And my older daughter is known as T. L. Bear.

Bear was seven years old, and had gotten to know my mom pretty well, but she had never met my father. She'd seemed interested in learning about him once or twice over the years, but I'd never told her much. I guess part of me had never forgiven him for his suicide. Like any girl, I'd wanted my dad to see my wedding and admire my children. But he hadn't. Diabetes be damned . . . hell, I had a right to be angry. Why couldn't he hang in there? Was he truly a coward? That's what Ernest had called their father when Clarence Hemingway killed himself.

I sat beside the crib, twisting the covers into my fist until I saw what I was doing. I stood up and straightened the blanket. Pookie slept on. For the first time it occurred to me just how much emotional baggage I still carried from my father's death. And now, in the shadow of my mother's passing, all my anger and sorrow was coming out. At her death I had understood how much Mom had missed Dad. That was part of the pain I felt—and resented. But for his own act, Dad could have been there. His suicide seemed all the more weak and selfish.

I had no way of knowing, as I left the nursery and went

back to the estate's paperwork, that I was about to rediscover my father's courage.

As for my older daughter, Bear was about to learn what it was like growing up in the Hemingway family. She would discover a grandfather and great-uncle she had never known, and solve a mystery that was perhaps even greater to a sensitive animal-loving child: why her family hunted.

ONE

I REMEMBERED the bright-purple Barney tape player in my older daughter's bedroom, and went looking for it, determined to listen to the tape. I found Bear in her room, curled up with a book about—ironically enough, it would turn out—endangered species.

"Hi, Mom," she said, barely looking up from a picture of a Siberian tiger.

"Hello, sweetie," I said, sitting down on the bed beside her. I picked up the Barney tape player. "I wonder if I could borrow this."

T. L. Bear made a face. She had recently "outgrown" Barney as a result of ridicule at school. "I don't care," she said. "He's the only animal I'm glad is extinct." She looked curiously at the cassette tape in my hand. "What's that?"

"I'm not sure," I said. "Something of Grandma's."

Bear sat up. "Can I hear it, too?" she asked eagerly. Grandma had been her best friend, and she felt the loss very deeply. Only her conviction that reincarnation was real made the death bearable at all.

"Of course," I said. I popped the tape in and punched Play.

Suddenly my Dad's voice crackled out of the speaker as if he were standing in the room. I was so startled I dropped the tape player. "My God," I said. "It's Daddy. . . ."

Bear picked up the machine, pushed the Stop button, and put it back on the bed. "Was that Grandpa?" she asked.

"Yeah," I answered. There was no mistaking the energy in his voice, the way he charged every word with excitement. "That's him, all right," I told Bear, taking her hand. "You never met him, but I think he would have liked you."

She smiled and said, "I want to hear him." I punched Play and we both fell back on her bed. It had been almost fifteen years since I had heard my father's voice, but when I closed my eyes it seemed like Daddy was right there with us.

I crouched there at the bank of the creek and felt the water trickling into one boot. Nothing seemed terribly wrong. The fall I'd taken seemed lucky now. I had more cover than Papa, who was working around to the other side. When he was in position, he would signal me and we would close in on our unlucky bear. Then I caught sight of the black bulk plainly in the alder thicket fifty yards ahead. A little closer and I would have a clean shot.

SUDDENLY THE CASSETTE STOPPED. "Wait a minute," my daughter said. She held her finger on the Stop button. "You didn't say they killed animals."

"Well, I don't really know what's on this tape," I said. She still glared at me. "All right. I know they hunted small stuff," I told her. "Dad talked about hunting birds with his brother— and they always ate what they killed." She looked at me in horror. "Oh, come on, Bear. You eat chicken, it's not that different." She rolled her eyes. I could see this wasn't going to be easy.

"He said 'bear,' " my daughter said firmly. "You know how I feel about bears, Mom."

I looked around at the dozens of stuffed animals in her room. Most of them were, in fact, bears. Sure, there were a few other animals—a tiger, a dog, a porpoise, a bird, a snake, a monkey, and a half dozen others—but bears made up the bulk of her collection. It was how she had earned her nickname. It was an odd coincidence that the first thing we heard on the tape was a story about her totem animal.

"Bears, Mom," she said again for emphasis.

"Yeah, well, it was different back then," I said, but she shook her head. It sounded feeble even to me. Killing animals for sport was wrong. It was clear to her, maybe to most people nowadays. So how could I explain a family that spent most of its free time hunting and fishing, when she had been raised to respect all living creatures and, above all, to be careful?

"Look, darling," I started, "the 1930s were a very different time. People didn't think about endangered species. People hunted for the sport—for the thrill."

"That's just so gross," she said.

I shrugged. "Well, if this tape is going to bother you, you don't have to listen."

"No, no, that's not what I meant. I want to hear the story. It's just that—" Bear made a face.

"Okay then, just save judgment until we hear everything," I said, and then it occurred to me: I had to do the same. I had questions too, but mine were more personal, and a lot harder to answer.

I pushed the Play button, hoping to find the answer.

My eyes moved back down to my rifle barrel. There was mud on the last three inches. My heart hammered. If what I suspected was true, I knew that missing my footing on the edge of this creek might have just cost me my life.

Papa was too far away to signal without the bear becoming aware of both of us. He would no doubt be mad as hell if he saw my gun. If our father had taught us anything, it was to take good care of hunting rifles.

I pulled the Springfield back with my right hand, wiped the muzzle with my left. With my clean hand I upended the rifle to make absolutely certain. There, where a .30-caliber hole should have been, a plug of mud filled the bore. Ah, hell, I thought. We're dead.

I was disarmed. Helpless. The rifle would explode if I fired without cleaning out the mud first. I had no knife and Papa's wouldn't do me any good. And less than fifty yards away, old Moccasin Joe, the massive black bear, clawed at our bait. With my rifle plugged with mud, I felt as helpless as a trapped animal.

Within minutes Papa would be close enough for the bear to smell him. Then the old he-bear would probably back off and head for me. Together we would have been a fair match for him. Papa was to hold his fire and back me up. This was how he had explained it and if you knew him, you knew you had to do as Papa told you.

Why had he given me first shot? Perhaps it was to see if his little brother had it in him—to see what I'd do when the bear charged. Of course, he added to the thrill when he warned me, "Old Joe there has the stuff to make hash out of both of us. Don't miss, Baron!"

Now, blast it, I had to get the mud out of my gun if I was ever to warm myself over a campfire again, not to mention stay in Papa's good graces. Which in itself was no easy trick. If I only had a cleaning rod. But I hadn't. Nor was there any sapling nearby that might reach the length of the barrel. There were alders up where the bear was, but I was damned if I was going to walk up to the bear with a useless gun and bat him on the head.

Carefully, my eyes on the bear, I crouched lower. I had one slim chance—better than doing nothing, but not by much. Slowly, ever so slowly, I eased the bolt up, and then back. There was a small snick as the bolt came back, bringing the cartridge out of the chamber. I put my hand over this cartridge and pocketed it. I heard it click against something else. With both hands holding my gun near the center of balance, I brought it up and tried to blow through the barrel. All I got was an oily taste. The mud didn't blow out, and that was that.

I STOPPED the tape player and looked at my daughter. I was worried about how my oversensitive child would take it all.

She frowned at me. "Hey, why did you do that? I want to hear what happened."

"Me too. I've never heard this story."

"Why not? Why didn't Grandpa tell you?" Bear asked.

"That's a good question. I guess it's just not the kind of story he told me."

"Then who did he tell?" she demanded.

I grabbed the orange-and-white-striped tiger from her animal collection. "Well, Tiger, I think there's only one place where my father would have told this story."

"Where?" my daughter asked.

"Do you remember Grandma's big old house in Miami Beach? The house I grew up in?"

Bear shook her head no.

"Well," I began, and my mind drifted back to my childhood home, a grand old estate. I could still picture the light from Dad's outdoor hearth dancing on the tan walls and across the red-tiled patio floor. "Sometimes in the evening, Grandpa would have a drink with friends and admire the sunsets over Biscayne Bay. The water was so beautiful in the light from the setting sun—blue-green, streaked with orange . . ."

"Miami?" Bear asked. "There's too many buildings."

I smiled. "Now there are. But back then, the Miami skyline's tallest building was the Freedom Tower. It was a beautiful place to grow up. And there was a circle of writers we knew. They'd get together and Dad would build a fire, and they'd have a few drinks and swap stories."

"A *fire*?" Bear chortled. "In *Florida*?"

"It was ceremonial." I smiled at her. "It gave everybody a sense of a special evening."

"Did it work?" she asked. "Really?"

"It sure did, honey," I nodded, thinking of the many people—writers and others—who approached me after my father's death, each with the same wistful glow on his face, and told me how special those gatherings were. "It really worked. This tape has to be from one of those evenings. I don't think he talked about Ernest much otherwise."

"Why not? Didn't he like him?"

"He liked him fine. Ernest was his big brother. He was sixteen years older than Dad, his hero when he was young. It's not that he had anything against him. Just that he didn't bring him up unless someone asked. I think—" I tried to sort it through in my own mind before answering. "I think your grandpa thought that the older-brother part of Ernest was special, something nobody else knew about, no matter how famous Ernest got. Maybe Daddy wanted to keep something for himself."

"Hey," my daughter interrupted, "this tape started halfway through. No wonder we're confused."

"No kidding. Here, let a professional fix it." I pulled the tape out of the machine and looked at the side on which my father's name was printed. "Whoops," I said. "Not only halfway through, but the wrong side. Let's flip it and start at the beginning." I turned the cassette over and put it back into the machine. I pressed Rewind, and for a moment we both just giggled. My daughter settled into my lap, and then I pushed Play.

Almost immediately my father's laughter filled the room. There was a sound that must have been the snap of pine crackling from the fire and we suddenly heard other voices. I listened until I made out who they were. There was the deep laugh of Charlie Willeford—Uncle Charlie was what my sister and I called him. Willeford was a Miami novelist whom I remember most for his warm good cheer and walrus mustache.

Also on the tape was the smooth cigarette-voice of my mother. And finally a mystery guest—someone I couldn't place. But there was a quality to his laugh that I didn't like. He always started to laugh a half-second after everyone else, as if he had been waiting to see if whatever was said was really funny. Or worse, as if he was waiting for permission—waiting to see if that's what Dad *wanted* him to do. And there was a practiced quality to the laugh, as if he had tried it out at home until it sounded the way he wanted it to. It was a lot to get from an old tape of a man's laugh, I know. But I didn't like him. I can't explain it any better than that.

A professor, I thought. *Another wannabe Hemingway aficionado.* But what the heck. Dad had had some strange guests over the years, from Jeane Dixon to Janet Reno. There were even some nice professors, like the guy who ran the art department at the University of Miami. Maybe I was wrong about this guy.

I tried to picture my old house as I listened to the tape. We had a lovely Spanish-style home filled with antiques, oriental rugs, and grand paintings. Of course as a child I thought this stuff was old and moldy and scary. But for the writers who visited, the house had a real mystique. Dad held his outdoor bonfires on a hibachi grill every Friday night, fueling it with dried pine and sea grape leaves. The group would stare out at Biscayne Bay and drink cocktails. When the sun set, they would toast the magical colors. That's when the stories would begin.

On the tape, the professor's voice came through unusually clear. "But Les, even on that last trip to Spain, Ernest seemed passionately devoted to that young bullfighter, Antonio Ordóñez. He sat for hours at his bedside."

"Oh Lord, here we go," I heard my mother mutter before Dad jumped in.

"Here's the thing," my dad said patiently. "Papa was a great man for putting himself in the other person's position. I think, in a sense, he was trying to psych himself into being able to write something where he was a young bullfighter. He was trying to really get inside the kid's skin."

"So you don't believe that Ernest's preoccupation with a macho lifestyle masked any kind of latent homosexual—"

There was a loud laugh that stopped the professor. Charlie Willeford spoke up. "You poor bastard. You're hanging yourself."

And then my father's voice: "Oh balls, Charlie, you brought him here, so I'll be nice. God's truth man, Papa was not a homosexual. Latent or late-blooming."

"Hear, hear," my mother muttered.

"But he did have an enormous ability to care about both males and females—not in an erotic way but in a 'You are a fellow human being' way. And when he cared for somebody, he cared as completely as you can care for a human being."

The professor began again. "Forgive me, but ah—I just believe the reading public may have the wrong image of Papa. It's important for the hunting stories—"

Dad cut him off. "Only a damn fool pictures Papa in hot-pink anything. Do you understand me?" There was real heat in Dad's words.

"Of course, Les. Naturally. I only meant to say—"

"Is that clear, God damn it?"

"Yes, absolutely. Sorry, Les." The professor backed off.

"Good. Because it's important for you to remember that nobody ever called him Mama."

I heard Charlie chuckle and say, "Sic 'em, Les."

"Yes, I know, I apologize," the professor was saying.

"They called him Papa. It's not a nickname he chose. People chose it for him—they called him that because that's who he was. Totally masculine, a guy who cared about the people around him and tried to show them what he could, what he knew about. My brother taught me more about hunting, fishing, and fighting than our father ever did. He lived up to the name Papa—and all that it implied. Always."

"I'm sorry, I'll stick to hunting questions," the professor said in a voice that would have buttered toast. "I read your account of the rabbit shoot in your biography, *My Brother, Ernest Hemingway.*"

"Sure you did. Are you asking permission to steal it?"

"No, no, of course not. I would, of course, paraphrase."

"I see. I suppose you've got a tape recorder on now. Recording an interview doesn't make you a writer. It makes you a leech." There was a small round of snickers from the others in the group.

"Well—actually, I do have a recorder."

"Great. So much for live it, feel it, then write it." There was a pause. In the background somebody lit a match and then coughed—Mom lighting a cigarette? Then Dad went on to the professor, "You don't get out much, do you?"

"What's wrong, Les, don't trust that pasty Chicago glow?" Charlie laughed.

"Charlie, you're also an English teacher—remind me again why I put up with you?"

"You like my books."

"Damn right. Good books, too."

I could picture Dad in his sweat-soaked Cuban guayabera shirt standing by the fire. Massive arms folded, he'd be staring hard at this awkward and pale professor in the flickering light. He didn't mean to, but he looked just like his brother, with the salt-and-pepper beard, the broad Hemingway jaw, and those wide, muscular shoulders. "What do you think you're going to accomplish with that tape recorder, Doctor?"

"Well, I can't very well go back in time to hunt with Ernest. So I was hoping to capture you."

There was a giggle from Mom. "Les, don't be so hard on the man. We're all here for a good time. If the professor wants to advance his career, why not share a few of Papa's hunting stories? I think," she paused, "we could all enjoy it."

"Thank you, yes, that's very kind," the professor said.

Willeford made a strange throat-clearing noise that might have covered a snort of laughter. "Yes, you know how eager Hemingway fans can be. Go on, Les. Tell him about—the lost safari."

Lost safari? What were they talking about? I saw my daughter stare up at me, eyes aglow. I shrugged that I didn't know either, and we both leaned in a little to hear better.

"God damn it, Charlie—"

"What fun—please, let's hear it, Les," my mother added.

There was a pause. The fire crackled and somebody moved a chair. Then I heard a growling sound—my father. "All right, Herr Doktor Professor," my father finally said. "They've talked me into it. *Una noche de verdades oscuras.* You do speak Spanish, right?"

"Oh yes, certainly—*claro que sí.*" The professor gave a nervous laugh, his first genuine one. There was a rustling, probably caused by the pulling of the recorder from its hiding place.

Dad spoke into the mike. "Test—test, one, two, three. Okay, Doctor Sony? Where do you want me to start, Charles?"

"Crocodiles," Willeford said. He sounded as if he was coughing, and this time I was sure he was trying not to laugh.

"Yes, that's my favorite part," my mother chimed in. "Tell about the crocodiles, Les."

I smiled and looked at my daughter. She was listening intently to the tape. Almost as intently as she watched TV, with a far-off stare, taking in my father's words and seeing them in her mind. I wondered if she had caught on to what seemed obvious to me—that my mom and Uncle Charlie were setting up Dad. Dad didn't like the professor, that was clear. Mom and Charlie had figured that out and had decided to have some fun. This had to be some kind of joke.

"Uh—" I heard my father say. He cleared his throat. "All right, God damn it. Crocodiles." And I heard him take a breath. I could almost see his forehead furrow and his hands come up as they always did to help him tell a story.

It had been far too many years since I had heard my dad tell one of his famous stories—and as far as I knew, I had never heard this one. Something inside me fluttered. I settled back and listened.

TWO

INDEED, CROCODILES," Dad said. "Professor, I want you to think about this. What would you do if the only thing between you and a twenty-foot croc was a flashlight? An awkward thing you'd jury-rigged to the tip of your rifle?"

"I don't really think I would put myself in that position."

"Of course you wouldn't," Dad said, and he let that sink in for a second before he went on. "To be fair, though, most people wouldn't. But I did. And I can't close my eyes without seeing it. I was there, understand. Less than ten feet away from that croc. His eyes glowing in the reflection of that light. Eyes that were a foot apart on a twenty-foot-long body. I was so eager to make sure I got a clean shot—and it very nearly cost me my life."

"What about Ernest?" the professor interrupted.

"Oh Christ, are you going to tell this story?"

"No, sorry."

"You want the straight dope? I'm going to give you stories that Papa never made public. Never. So get the details right, sport." I heard ice rattle as Dad took another sip of his drink. Then he began.

A croc this length is a huge fellow, and he weighs half a ton easy. I've seen crocs that size skinned out by better hunters than Papa and I. And I've tried to lift just their tails. Those tails are more dangerous than their jaws, as you will see. But until that first night, when I finally learned how to approach a huge fellow whose skin was worth over a hundred thousand dollars, I never really knew what I'd do.

Charlie Thompson had taken sick and they'd sent him to a larger African village, one that had a hospital. That's why I got a telex from Papa to come join his group. I was just a twenty-year-old kid, I didn't think about the danger. And I didn't really know anything about big-game hunting. But in my family, we've always liked to learn things the hard way.

I got to East Africa just a few days after Papa's thirty-sixth birthday. He said my present to him was to help him land a really big croc. I kidded him about where to put the ribbon, but in truth, I had no idea how hard this hunt would be.

We spent a week shooting at and hitting a number of small five- to six-foot crocs. But we were getting very few skins, because we were shooting at such a distance. And we were absolutely unable to even get within range of the big fellows—the only ones really worth shooting, since skins were our top consideration.

See, Ernest had been delighted by the reports that the African papers had carried from time to time of the skill and daring of "B. Dempster," as the press called him, a pioneer professional crocodile hunter. Dempster, who was almost a legend, had been hunting the upper and lower stretches of the Zambezi for years. He'd shot thousands of big crocs, and though there were still any number more, the Zambezi had finally closed to commercial shooting when the great wildlife refuge was extended.

But that didn't deter us, or Dempster, for that matter. He simply took to hunting in Portuguese territory, in Angola, and he was a great success there as well. Well, Papa wanted to have Dempster's success, but he didn't want to go to Dempster himself. He had heard of a group who had done that and they didn't make out so well. Dempster was still shooting on the Zambezi, and though he'd offered to show them how, rumor was that they'd alienated him—hurt his feelings in some way—

and he would have nothing more to do with young hopefuls, or competition of any kind for that matter. Papa felt he understood Dempster better than any man alive.

At any rate, we never did see Dempster or talk with him. Papa thought about writing him, but then we heard he had become even more difficult. So we were on our own.

Papa decided we'd try the country further east. There was no restrictive legislation there and, starting in a small way, we hoped to learn by doing. We had only our guns, .303 Enfields, several hundred rounds of soft-nose cartridges, the camping outfit Papa had gathered together on the last safari, and enough money to buy a wooden dugout canoe.

That was where our education as crocodile hunters began. And that was where we found that before you can kill a croc, you must first kill, or outwit, the crocodile birds. For every time we'd leave camp and paddle upstream to the good sandbanks or float ever-so-silently down with the current to a wonderful marshy area only a couple of miles below our little clearing on the bank, these cursed white crocodile birds would give the warning, and all the big saurians would slide into the stream before we were within a quarter of a mile. Those birds are the permanent warning system of the fat reptiles of the world, and I've since heard they are the same in India, South America, and Australia.

We tried stalking our skins any number of ways. We used

a tan shelter half over Papa, placed up on the bank only a few yards from where we'd seen the big crocs come out of the water. But even when I went with him at dawn, and we could hear the pigeons cooing in the trees just behind the sand spit, he got into position all right, but the crocodile birds spotted him. They made such a fuss over him, and all up and down the sand bar, that none of the big skin-owners would come out of the water, and there we were, with no shot. He fired at the eyes of one, and only got a ricochet off the water.

Little crocs we could sometimes surprise, as we floated along the silent waterway, starting well upstream in the morning. The birds didn't seem to value them so much, and we nailed a few and were able to skin them out fairly well. But with the big ones—nothing. No luck at all. Those damned birds gave us away every time.

Finally, though, our big break came. We'd been doing so much plotting and getting so little in return that the natives had come down visiting, and talked with our head boy, a coastal native.

"Bwana," he says. "They ask why don't we hunt *nyo-koko* as did their forefathers."

"Ask them in what manner was that," Papa said. He was as fed up with our useless forays against the warning birds as I was.

Our head boy chatted back and forth with the visitors a little more. Then he said to Papa, "Bwana, it is a thing I never even knew. He says in the old days"—and he gestured as with a spear—"the big ones were always taken with torches, and assagai, in the middle of the night."

"You know, Baron," Papa said. That's what he called me. "That's a hell of a solution. Those damned birds are all high in the branches of some tree once it gets full dark. And the crocs have nothing to warn them, except their noses and imaginations, from dusk to dawn."

"We've nothing to worry about, with their imaginations," I said, and we silently shook hands, realizing that we had solved our biggest problem in technique.

But we still lacked good lights. There was no use in balling our way along, using hand torches, the way the old man had described early tribal hunts. We didn't have a lot of men, and without lots of men and torches, such a thing would only result in somebody being chopped in half before we could bring the guns to bear.

"We do have one chance though," Papa said. "We could tape that big flashlight of yours under your gun barrel, and drift in very close before turning it on."

"You thought of it, so you get first shot," I said.

"On the contrary, Baron, it's your light. Besides, if you'll continue to point with your weapon after you fire, I'll take second shot and make sure I don't lose my only kid brother."

Anyway, that's what we thought, and that's how it stood,

when we made a late afternoon survey of the several sand bars down near the river mouth the first day. Neither of us realized then just how crazy it was to try this stunt, with no outboard motor, no one else in the cranky dugout to help paddle, and no experience in locating the vital brain area on a monster croc-odile by the wiggling rays of a flashlight.

That evening we discussed, or rather, Papa talked about, the hunt into the late hours. He called our head boy over. He was a good native tracker and understood we didn't have shillings enough to hire a whole group of fishermen from the coastal settlement down the way, and approach the big crocs at night with plenty of torches and spears. We wanted him to come in the dugout with us, and we'd try it the small way, down by the first big sand bar where lots of the debris from the river washed in, and the shallows made it easy for the crocodiles to get their fill of fish.

"No, bwana," our head boy told him. "If anyone wishes to do this thing, he may. But I hunt only in daylight, and I fish only in daylight, unless I am with many people and only on dry land. Night is when the water spirits take over."

This was Papa's translation, and coming from a local resi-dent, it made sense. The local fishermen of the coast were poor, used primitive equipment, and took their losses from crocodiles every year, among them the women who gathered water and washed clothes down by the clear streams.

"This one's going to be our own show, Baron," Papa said to me, and I agreed. We both knew that if it worked, we'd have access to at least one of the larger crocs every night, and that would bring us in plenty of skins and some damned fine stories, in short order.

The professor interrupted. "So Papa knew you wanted to be a writer?"

"Hell, yes. He was pretty proud that I had won a national short story contest in high school. My name wasn't on it, so he called it an honest award."

"Did he pass down any words of wisdom?"

"He said, 'Baron, if you're serious about wanting to be a writer, you have a hell of a road ahead. Everything you do will be compared to my work. But if you're going to be a writer, then write. And remember when something gives you the emotional shakes, figure out exactly what shook you. Remember every detail. If anybody is around, find out if they were shaken too and how much and why. The more sides you can see to any story, the more you will know.' "

Dad paused, then added, "No more interrupting, Leech—understand?" The professor must have agreed, because Dad continued.

We drifted downriver to the first huge crocodile. I remembered the stories our head boy had told Papa about crocs felled by dozens of spears in the old days that, when they were opened up, had been found to have brass bracelets in their stomachs, identified as belonging to members of families who had disappeared down near the stream. This big one was almost certainly an eater of men. He couldn't have lived so long and grown so big without having had his share. But we'd fix him in a moment. The heavy, musky odor was strong in my nostrils as he glared balefully at my light. The current moved us slowly along and when we were less than fifteen feet away, and still coming toward him, Papa whispered, "Now!"

If we'd waited until we were the same distance downstream as we were upstream from our quarry, what happened then might never have occurred. But everyone knows how to do a thing properly afterward, and no man could have foreseen the immediate happenings. My front sight was notched down in the V and rested right between the eyes of the beast. I knew Papa was aiming at the same time, and waiting only to hear my rifle before he fired. I squeezed the trigger, and in the instant, felt the roar of the .303 shooting down at the target less than ten feet away.

The bullet made a slight white gash, right between the eyes, and then Papa's rifle sounded in my ear and I saw another flick of scale several inches behind mine. And then the croc's body seemed to rise up on his front legs—indeed it did rise, and he came up in the air in a somersaulting twist right toward us. The dugout lay across the line of his fall. I instinctively raised my rifle across me to ward off the blow. I had only a momentary glimpse of the stars in the deep blue before the great black shape came over on us like a wet pile-driver and then everything was black.

I came to with struggling movements, floundering in the water. I was moving my feet, treading-fashion, and weakly paddling with my hands. I couldn't seem to breathe and yet I knew I was on the surface. I could hear Papa calling my name, "Baron, Baron." I spat convulsively. The muddy taste of river water mixed with bile and blood in my mouth, but I finally managed to say, "What?"

"Where are you?" Papa said.

I tried to say I didn't know. Something between a moan and a grunt came out instead. I brought my right hand up to my face. Something was wrong. "Try and come over this way," Papa said. I got the direction of the sound, but couldn't see anything. I moved lazily, as in a swimming dream, and then, suddenly, I remembered what had happened.

For all I knew the giant croc was still nearby, eyeballing my legs. I suppressed another moan, and gently sidestroked to the sound of Papa's voice. Then I was touching bottom, and staggering ashore into Papa's arms.

"We've the luck of the Irish, brother," he said. "The river

has more crocs than we can use right now, and we're at last on this sand bar." Then, his eyes focusing in the dark, he got a close look at my face. "Christ," he said, and repeated, "the absolute luck of the Irish. With the blood coming out of you, and that blow you had, it's amazing you're breathing, Baron." He led me up the bank and away from the water and then down the sand bar to where driftwood had piled up, and I lay down. He tied off the bleeding gash with strips of his shirt, then gathered some stout sticks to use for clubs, and stood guard over me until dawn.

Later that day, when our head boy had gotten a raft made and took us off the sand bar, and we'd sent out word to watch for the freighter that had brought us to the river's mouth, I went delirious. Papa saved my life, for I was trying to claw at the rough bandages he'd fitted over my mashed nose and face. A swift punch put me out. I didn't come to until I was in the hospital in Dar es Salaam, and again Papa was with me when I came around.

"That was the grandfather of all crocs to try for, and we got him for sure," he said. "But we shot him on both sides of the brain, and not dead-center like we'd hoped. He nearly had you, Baron. Smashed your rifle right into your face, busted our dugout, lost us both our guns, and gave me a sweat bath as well as a river one swimming back to shore. We were close to being eaten that night. But don't worry, kid. We'll do it better next time. We're professionals now, Baron. We've had our blood-bath."

That's when he held out a two-inch croc tooth and handed it to me. "A souvenir, kid, a little something I pulled from your rifle butt."

THREE

T HERE WAS a pause on the tape. For a moment I wasn't sure if the tape was over, but then I heard a noise: Charlie Willeford clearing his throat. My daughter straightened up and gave me a look. "Your daddy was brave."

"Sure, sure he was—if it's true." I tried to force a smile. I didn't want to shatter the image of a really cool grandfather. And there were a lot of things I loved about my dad—but I still couldn't shake my last image of him. Not on the basis of one crocodile story.

It had been a typical hot, muggy Florida day.

Dad, sitting in his boxer shorts at the dining table, was crying because his legs were cold. Sounds silly now, but I should have known how wrong it was. My father had not been a man to complain. If we were sailing in gale-force winds, he would say, "Don't sweat it, kid." And he'd pull in the mainsheet and send our little boat leaping over mountainous blue waves.

But in his last three months he'd had four failed surgeries to restore circulation in his legs. His battle with Type II diabetes was drawing to a quick end. Doctors had scheduled him for a double amputation.

I remember arguing that he shouldn't give up. Then he just stopped the suicide talk. And the next day he took the "family exit." That's what he called it, after his father and brother ended their lives that way. I still called it suicide, and I'd never told my daughter. The one time she'd asked about her grandfather, I'd said, "Your grandpa got sick and died." Now here he was again, alive, at least in voice, and telling of great and exciting adventures. How could I take that away from her?

"Nobody makes up a story like that," she said, and I gave her a small hug.

"There was an awful lot of good detail," I agreed, "but your grandfather *did* make up stories sometimes and he was really good at it."

"Okay, Mom, tell you what. If he comes back on and says 'Got you,' I'll believe he made it up."

"And if not, then what?" I asked.

"If not, then you should make a book out of it." She had that light in her eyes again, and I shook my head. I didn't want to discourage her, but—

"Bear," I said, "if only it was that easy. It takes more than just one good story to make a book."

"Listen to the rest of the tape, Mom. Maybe the rest will be there."

I laughed. At least I'd found that hunting stories could fly with a new generation. Maybe the Hemingway Tradition wasn't dead after all.

The Professor's voice came up next. He couldn't restrain himself, and began, "So did you and Papa go back?"

"For crocs? No," Dad answered. "By the time I was out of the hospital, Papa had heard of a new sport he wanted to try. He had been hunting in the Serengeti with Charles Thompson, who had recovered before I did. Papa had replaced our lost .303s with .30–06 Springfield rifles. He always had success shooting with heavier loads. He'd killed two buffalo and his lion. He had come to have tremendous faith in the gun's accuracy and shocking power, even with the most dangerous sort of African game."

"Which were?" the professor asked.

"Aw, not the wild ostriches," Willeford said. "I was going to use that some day."

"Bastard," my father rumbled.

"Ostriches?" the professor said. "You mean the birds?"

"They're awfully *big* birds," I heard my Mom chime in. "But Les doesn't like to tell that story."

"I'd love to hear it, though," the professor said. "Ostriches were never mentioned in any of Ernesto's African books."

"*Wild* ostriches," Charlie corrected. "Bigger, meaner, quicker than you can imagine, right Les?"

"Please, Les," the professor said. "I mean—if you wouldn't mind. Why didn't Ernest ever mention these animals? Especially if they really are so ferocious—" Even I could hear the condescending amusement in the man's voice. So could my dad, apparently; he pounced on the man.

"What do you mean 'if,' Professor?"

"I, I—I just meant, really, you know . . . they're just ostriches, aren't they?"

I heard my father say softly, "You think you're so clever nothing can hurt you, is that it?"

"Er . . . No, not really," the professor said in a very small voice. I pictured Dad towering above a pasty little ferret.

"You're still thinking it's just a bird," Dad said. "But so is a fighting cock. Did you ever see a cockfight, Professor?"

"Well, um, I've certainly heard many stories. . . ."

"I'll bet you have. And do you understand that pound for

pound a fighting cock is the meanest, toughest animal on the face of the earth?"

"That is, ah—certainly consistent with what I've heard."

"Good. I'm happy for your consistency. I toast your consistency." I heard the clink of ice cubes. "And now I want you to picture a lightning-fast fighting cock over eight feet tall, weighing three hundred pounds and raised in the wild Kalahari Desert, where only the toughest, most vicious animals can survive."

"I, I, um, hadn't pictured it quite so vividly—" the professor stuttered.

"Goddamned right you hadn't," my father said.

"Please, Les, tell the story. I mean, if you wouldn't mind."

There was a long pause. "All right," my father finally said, and I heard a round of throat-clearing from Charlie and Mom.

"You have to understand," my father began, "my brother was a damned proud man. He looked at this more as a potential business deal. An adventure, sure, but a way out, too. Very few people knew how desperately he wanted to leave Key West to live in Africa. Of course Pauline would never have agreed, but had the ostrich venture worked out, it would nevertheless have happened, no matter what the risk."

The professor interrupted. "But surely, hunting ostriches can't possibly be as dangerous as fighting bulls, stalking lions, or fishing for blue marlin?"

"Dangerous? What the hell do you know about dangerous,

Professor? Haven't you heard a goddamned word I said? You think because you've never seen a wild ostrich attack that it's just a big bird. But a lot of men have gone up against them thinking that, and all I can say is, it is a novel way to die. Now am I going to tell this or not?"

"Oh, by all means, sorry, go ahead," the professor said. I heard a chair scrape, and the clink of a glass followed by a satisfied, "Ahh."

Then my father began.

I thought I had seen it all and done quite a bit of it, until I stood there sweating, naked to the waist and breathing hard, under the blazing-hot African sun. If Papa had known what we were in for I don't think he would have done it. Like you, he'd assumed that the wild ostrich was just a big bird, and the stories we'd heard about their ferocity were intended to frighten us, have a little fun with the white hunters. As I said, he was a fiercely proud man, and once he thought that, he had to show them all.

And so there we were.

And we had learned fast that the Kalahari ostrich is one mean, tough bird. We had to be a little tougher and meaner, and of course, we'd need our luck, too, all the luck we could get. I was about to find out just how dangerous the cock ostrich can be when your luck runs out.

We'd been rounding up ostrich for a week. Papa had fallen in love with Africa, and Charlie Thompson had suggested raising these rugged birds as a way to make money with the land. Papa had said I could be in for half the profits if I pulled my own weight. Of course, I soon came to realize just what that meant, and that I might not be around to enjoy any profits.

We had come up to the Kalahari Desert on the eastern edge of southwest Africa. We had hired out horses for enough time to do the job—three weeks. We had decided that we would either cable success and send for more funds to bring the birds home or keep silent and admit defeat only to ourselves.

We knew there had been a scientific expedition up there recently on the edge of the desert. They had reported seeing occasional groups of wild ostriches, truly feral birds unlike anything you can imagine. The scientists' plane had dived at five or six birds gathered together, and they had observed the females with immature plumage sticking their heads in the sand.

"That doesn't prove a thing," Papa said. "I asked a guy who had an ostrich farm about it—he said they don't hide when scared—said they were just hunting for grub when they buried their heads in the sand—and he ought to know."

"So how are we going to catch these fowl?" I asked, changing the subject.

"I figured we'd ask the locals this time," Papa said. "They must have figured it out—since they live at the edge of this godforsaken sea of cactus."

We asked. And we got quite a few horror stories about the big birds, which Papa continued to ignore. We were given many offers by locals to help chase the birds—but it always ended up in a debate about how many eggs per nest would be theirs. And so after a half-dozen conversations that followed the same track of thinking, Papa decided to ignore the "experts."

"Either they don't know, or they're not telling," he said to me. "I say we just head out and try our luck."

"Fine," I said. "They're just big birds, aren't they?" It was one of those offhand, cheerful goddamned remarks that come back to haunt you, and I wish I had never said it. But I did, and Papa agreed, and we headed for the country where the feral ostriches were plentiful.

We had read the ancient accounts of how the first ostrich hunters had sighted and captured their original specimens of adult birds, and so it wasn't long before Papa and I began scoring. It broke down into a two-part hunt. First you had to get the big birds tired, and then you had to capture them. Both stages had their dangers.

By the second day out, we had gotten one female, and the third day another, and so on until in three weeks, counting our failures and difficult runs where we lost our quarry, we had three young cocks and six females, in all stages of development, from two-year-old chicks to beautiful mature birds. Perhaps reading those old accounts had helped us more than we knew; we had learned things that modern ostrich farmers in Africa didn't seem to know—or at least they had never found them out the hard way, which is the only way to learn something and make it stick.

There's an old African saying that a full-grown ostrich will wear out two horses. One of the first things we learned was that this was true. By the second day we had hit on the idea to single out a bird and to divide into two chase parties. That way we could usually run it down, in two one-hour relays during the daylight hours. Of course we never knew just what shape the bird was in at the beginning of the chase. We just always assumed we would win and in more than two-thirds of our daily runs we caught what we went after.

We'd start out in the early morning light, when the desert is most fascinating—and most habitable. There are few spots in this world that are so lovely in the early morning. The worst of the night chills are over and the colors are clearer than they are anywhere else. Every tiny plant seems to be sucking up the moisture you feel in the air. You can see tiny droplets on the leaves and shoots of the scarce and scattered wild flowers. You know that in just an hour they will be shining and dry and their wait-a-bit blossoms will stand ready. That is when they look as if they have been there forever and you know that you are the stranger, and always will be.

Morning after morning we went from our outpost and

raised one or two birds—sometimes more because it was mating season. Invariably we singled out one and made it the chase for the day. We had been awfully lucky so far. Each time we roped our bird, we'd blindfolded it and brought it back to the native corral we were using as a holding pen.

It had all gone well, amazingly well, and we were down to wanting only one more bird, and knew we would get it. On this last morning we'd gone over to where we had sighted so many small groups. There were literally hundreds of the big birds in this desert area, more than three hundred miles north of Cape Town, yet not officially in the Kalahari Desert park. All the desert proper had been put out of bounds, and that was an area we stayed dead clear of. Instead we worked off to the south and west, right down along the border where there were occasional stagnant pools of water which we knew the ostriches used. It was still illegal to be there. You had to have a permit. But permits took months, time we didn't have.

Still, Papa was wary. As a young man, he had shot a bird illegally in Michigan. The lesson he learned came from our Uncle George. Uncle George lived in a neighboring county and Ernest had figured he'd be safe beyond jurisdiction of local law. But Uncle George showed no trace of sympathy. He advised Ernest to turn himself in and pay the fine. Papa did this, and it helped him form his own code of behavior.

Papa believed that only people who would help you in a jam were of value, and all others were worthless. It seemed to me I had been put to the test to prove my value on this big bird hunt. Papa had cut out a handsome bird and gone racing up a hill with the cock just ahead of him.

"I'll concentrate on the bird," Papa called as he rode by me where I sat on my horse. "Be ready at the far end when I ride by. You give the final lap and I'll be ready when you get him back to me."

And so it went. I did my part, and when Papa drove the bird to me I picked up the chase. But the ostrich was not co-operating. It would not stop, not even slow down. It just wouldn't tire. I chased it across the blazing desert floor until my horse was starting to blow. It didn't seem possible that Papa and I could have been chasing this bird for more than two hours at a full gallop. But we had.

And finally my own mount gave out, after the weary long gallop down a gully, before I'd been able to drive the bird back to where Papa and his horse were getting their second wind. I could picture Papa, winded and panting, wishing we had never even started on this god-awful rugged path to fortune. If we got this last ostrich, we'd have ten, and that would be the start of our ranch. But we were still very far from getting him into our corral.

I finally slowed my exhausted mare to a walk. To continue the chase might kill her. And to my great relief, after spurting ahead of us for about a hundred yards, the ostrich finally stumbled to a stop, too, and keeled over. I rode slowly up and brought my weary mount to a stop not twenty feet away. I grabbed the lasso and swung down, intending to walk over and get a hitch around the bird's feet, so he could take no long steps, either in running or kicking. That was the way we had taken the others. Once roped, we pulled a sock over the head and then led or dragged them back to the corral.

But when I got within a few feet, this big bird gave a heave and rose to its knees. That wasn't good. The bird wasn't as winded as my horse and I, and he might bolt again at any moment. I pulled at the loop in my lasso and tried to open it wider, intending to flip it over him right from there. That sudden motion, seen from the corner of his eye, did it. As I shook out the loop, the bird rolled. I lofted out the loop and it caught just for a moment on his far-side wing. Then he stood up and the weight of his action jerked the rope right out of my hand. I felt a sudden burning sting on my palms and saw the rope whip away—but I didn't have time to think about that.

Because it was then that the giant cock, beautiful bird that he was, turned on me. And I knew I was in trouble.

He walked toward me and I found myself retreating. His massive body was delicately balanced on the two pole-like legs, and his thin neck towered upward a good two feet over my head. He seemed awkward, yet mechanically competent as he came at me with his pistonlike steps.

As I said, I knew I was in trouble, and I had no idea what to do about it. I was all alone on the floor of the gully. Papa couldn't see down here, and I had no idea how far away he was. I had lost the rope and my rifle was with my horse, which might as well have been back in Cape Town. I had no weapon beyond my pocketknife, and this bird looked far from exhausted as he stalked toward me.

I undid the first three buttons of my shirt, then ripped off the last two and took the shirt off—so I would have something in my hand when he tried to deliver his lethal kick. A shirt against a kick that could disembowel a lion. How I wished for a "tacky," one of those clubs with the spiny mimosa the professional breeders have on the ostrich farms. They are used for defense against just such cocks as these when they are in *quei,* or mating frenzy. I remembered some of the stories about the savageness of the ostrich cock in the breeding season and how it had caused so many fatalities. They had told us that a cock in *quei* will attack anyone or anything. Suddenly the stories did not seem so farfetched.

The giant bird stopped short a few steps away from me and uttered his weird cry. There were two short *boo*s and then a loud *boom.* It came from deep in his throat. On the boom, his wings widened out and he charged, hissing. As he came on I crouched, ready to launch myself at him. I knew only one thing. I wasn't going to give him a chance to de-gut me with that great evil spiked toe of his.

I stared at the bird's huge feet, only two steps away from me now, and at the ugly head hissing almost in my face. Then he took the final step forward and I saw which leg he was going to stand on. I lurched forward, arm and flapping shirt ready to cover the birds head—when I lost my balance and sprawled at his feet. I pulled my legs up to protect my abdomen.

But he didn't strike. My forward motion had thrown the bird into evasive action. He suddenly needed his kicking leg to stand on. As it came back under him, I scrambled up, shirt still in hand. The bird turned to circle around again.

As he moved in to attack, I knew that this time the shirt wouldn't frighten him. But when he was still several yards away, he turned and stood hissing at something over my shoulder. I didn't dare take my eyes from the bird to look, but I wondered what could scare this cock enough to cause him to break off an attack?

I got my answer soon enough.

"Baron," I heard my brother say from perhaps a hundred feet off, "don't give up, you've almost got him."

"Or he's almost got me," I called back, still not daring to look away.

"Christ, don't quit now," Papa said. "I could help you, but if you catch him yourself, it will mean a hell of a lot more."

Now I know a sane man might have questioned Papa's reasoning here, but hey, I was the kid brother. I did what I was told. I know now I should have tried to lure the bird over to my lasso. But the adrenaline was pumping. I had escaped the daggers of his feet the first time, and my only thought was to escape them once again. But how?

Then I had a flash of inspiration. I needed to use something else. I had only pants and boots on. But I had a belt!

"I'll feed this damn beast my belt," I said aloud.

"Now you're thinking, kid," Papa said from the safety of his horse, still a good fifty feet away.

The giant bird had decided that Papa was no immediate threat, and started hissing at me again. But he hadn't taken more than five of those pistonlike steps before I was unfastening the shiny buckle.

The cock must have figured it was going to be him or me, for he lengthened his stride as he charged this time. His head was extended well out, hissing. He was far from being the winded bird I had thought I could rope and capture without Papa's help only a few minutes earlier.

"It's now or never," I told myself, and whipped out the belt full length. I held the shirt in one hand and the belt in the other as the three-hundred-pound cock came malevolently on. I hefted the belt, buckle out, to flip it toward his head.

I stood poised with my belt and shirt. I knew I would have to get in awfully close—perhaps too close. But it was my best chance. The belt felt good in my right hand. The shirt was bunched and wadded in my left, ready to fly out and make him close his eyes—if I used it just right.

He was only a step away—fifteen feet for one of his steps—when he stopped for the fateful kick.

"Watch his feet, he'll telegraph his kick," Papa called, as if he was coaching a boxer. That was when I jumped again. But this time I wasn't quite as lucky. The single talon of the huge toe arced out and caught the outer edge of my right thigh as I shot to the left. In the fastest one-two motion of my life, I flashed the shirt in his face and swung the belt and buckle at his neck.

This time the bird and I went down together. I frantically grabbed his neck in both arms and felt his mighty body thrash around sideways on the ground. He was hard to hold. Twice the neck almost twisted out of my grasp like some uncanny snake.

"Birds are just giant reptiles," Papa yelled from his horse.

"This SOB is a boa constrictor," I hollered back, holding on to the neck with a death grip. Then his head popped out from under the shirt. There was a lightninglike slash at my head and I heard, as well as felt, the flesh of my ear tear. A warm wash of blood came down my face and neck and seemed to soothe my nerves. I got his head tucked under again. The spiny feathers of that long agile neck were repulsive to me, but I pulled his head down to my chest and disentangled the belt. Then I got on my knees and began to knot the shirt securely. All the time I sat on his body, with my legs tucked under his soft, plumed wings and belly, so that his powerful limbs kicked uselessly out behind.

In the distance I heard a thudding—but I wasn't sure whether it was the blood in my torn ear or not. As I finished the third knot, I saw Papa come riding in closer. I stayed just as I was, breathing hard and knowing how lucky I was to be alive.

"Good work," Papa called as he approached. "How did that feel?"

"This would bring a whole new meaning to cockfighting in the Keys," I called back, seeing Papa come slowly down the hill so that his horse would not spook the bird.

"You're right. We'd make a fortune. Just as long as you don't get yourself killed."

I shook my head to clear it. I could feel the blood running down onto my chest from the torn ear.

"You all right, Baron?" Papa said as he rode up. There was real concern in his tone. He looked at me again and squinted unbelieving. "You're hurt, kid. Why didn't you say so?" He jumped down and came running over.

He looked at the side of my head and at my pants, where the bird had slashed through, gashing my thigh. "My God, man, we've got to get something on that." He went back to his horse and got both his rope and a bottle of gin he had in the saddlebag. In a few seconds he had a good short length of rope between the cock's legs. He then crouched on the bird and said, "Bend down, you bum." In two sure strokes he doused the left side of my head and my right thigh with the alcohol. I could feel the burning working its way in. "That ought to fix you. As for our friend here . . ." He pulled out a sock and slipped it over the cock's head.

I stared at the awesome creature still jerking, trying to kick even though he was muffled and hobbled and sat upon by Papa. His black-and-white plumage glistened in the desert sun. "He put up a good fight, Papa. Maybe he deserves a better chance," I spoke up.

"Nonsense," Papa cut in. "To the victor—belongs the ostrich. Besides, he's going to have the time of his life fathering the most magnificent chicks on our ranch. Would you deny him that? Just because he tried to tear your guts out, kid?"

I laughed then. It hurt, but I managed. "Okay," I told my brother, "let's get our wild flock back to civilization."

"Excuse me," the professor interrupted on the tape. "But I know that Ernest never moved to Africa—so what happened to your ranch?"

I could hear my father take a sip of a drink. "Pauline, as I said, did not want to move her family to Africa. And after Ernest saw the wounds on me, he started having second thoughts about raising three sons in the company of such vicious birds. So we sold all ten and split the profits."

"What did you do with your hard-earned loot?" Charlie Willeford asked.

"Well, there was still an area of Africa that Papa wanted to explore. He said it would make up for all my trouble on our other adventures."

The tape hissed and crackled. Then the door to my daughter's bedroom opened and I turned off the tape player.

FOUR

JEFFRY CAME into the room and sat at the foot of the bed holding Miss Pookie. "How are my girls?" he whispered, brushing the hair from my cheek to give me a kiss. He then turned to kiss Bear's forehead, and passed Pookie over to me for her breast-feeding.

"We're great, Daddy!" Bear answered.

I smiled, and for some reason Pookie looked up and smiled at the same time. "The tape," I said, looking from Pookie's sweet face to my husband. "The tape from Mom's safe-deposit box. It has Daddy telling a bunch of stories to some English professor."

"That's good," he said.

"Yeah, it is, but—these are very bizarre stories, Jeff."

"What did you expect? He never told a dull one that I heard of."

Jeff and his family had been friends with my family for over thirty years, and most of Jeff's childhood memories of my family were about my father. I'd just been an annoying hyperactive kid. But Dad had left a lasting impression wherever he went.

"Jeff, remember when we were kids and our families went on that camp-out down in the Keys?"

"Sure. Your dad told a fantastic story about pirate treasure on the drive down. I almost climbed over into the front seat trying to hear better."

"Exactly. I have a vague memory of that story, but I clearly recall digging up most of the beach at Harry Harris Park. I wanted that treasure."

"What's your point?" Bear asked.

"The point is, your father and I know how convincing your granddad was—and I just don't want you to get your hopes up about these stories."

"It didn't hurt you, did it?" Jeff asked me. "What are you really worried about?"

"I don't know," I admitted.

"Daddy," Bear chimed in, "we're going to publish these stories."

"Really?" Jeff raised an eyebrow. "They'd have to be pretty good."

"They are, they are, they are," Bear responded.

"If only it was that easy," he said.

"That's just what Mommy said." She giggled.

Jeffry smiled. "Well, she's right. There's a long road between a good story and a good book."

"But you and Mom write books all the time," Bear insisted. "And these stories are *really* good!"

Jeffry looked at me. "Are they?"

"Well—" I paused. "There's a lot of detail, but—I don't think they're true. Still, they're funny as hell."

"I even like them and I really hate hunting," Bear added.

"But what if these stories *are* true?" Jeff asked.

I waited to answer. "Oh, they can't be. I mean, I would have known."

"Would you? Do you think Bear here knows everything I did?" He turned to our daughter. "I used to play lead guitar in a rock band."

"Really? Cool." Bear grinned.

"Look," I said. "Maybe I don't know everything my father did. He did have a life before children. But these stories—I mean, what we've heard so far—"

"They're too cool not to be true," Bear said.

"Sometimes that means they're not," Jeff said, ruffling his daughter's hair. But when he saw her expression he added, "But maybe they are. Who knows?"

"Well," I said, lifting Pookie up on my shoulder to burp her. "Why don't you listen and see what you think?"

Jeff grinned. "Thought you'd never ask." He nodded at Bear. "Play it, Sam."

I laughed and watched as Bear reached over and started the cassette. All of us sat back and listened as my father's voice once again filled the room.

"—he was talking about?" the professor asked. We had missed a few words. I moved to hit the Rewind button, but Jeffry and Bear waved me away in unison, grinning at each other like a pair of goons.

"Oh, it's not all that important," my father said on the tape.

"But I would really love to hear it," the professor insisted. "I mean, if you don't mind."

"I've already talked too much," my father said. "Besides, there's a pretty good sunset about now."

On the tape we could hear people shifting position, feet scuffing on the patio floor. "It's beautiful," my mother said. "Look at the rose-colored light across the bay."

"There's no other sunset like that in the world," my father said.

"Oh, I don't know," Charlie Willeford said thoughtfully. "That isn't what you told us."

"What the hell are you talking about?" my father said.

"Don't be so damned modest, Les," Willeford said. "I know you said it's not all that important, but it's a great story. The desert with your brother. At sunset. Where was it—was it East Africa?"

"God damn it, Charlie," my father began.

"Oh, yes, tell that one, Les," my mother said happily. "Tell about the monkeys."

"Not monkeys, God damn it," my father said.

"Of course not," agreed Willeford. "They were baboons."

"Baboons—really?" the professor chimed in breathlessly. "What on earth was Ernest doing hunting baboons?"

"He wasn't hunting baboons," my father snarled. "The baboons were hunting me! And they damned near got me, too!"

"Made a monkey of you, didn't they?" my mother murmured in her soft, throaty voice. I heard what must have been Uncle Charlie choking back laughter. Then the professor plodded on.

"But baboons are completely harmless, gentle communal primates that—"

"Gentle!" my father exploded. "They near as Christ gentled me to death. Don't feed me your academic fairy tales. I've been there and I know different. Baboons gentle. Jesus Christ."

"Of course, Les, sorry. That's just what I'd read. But Ernest was there, too? Is that right, Les?"

"Ernest was *not* there," Daddy said. "And it wasn't sunset, either. It was high noon, and it was hotter than Hades. And I truly believed that I would never see another sunset. Even now, it's hard to believe how it happened."

"There's a cue-line," Charlie Willeford muttered.

"How *did* it happen, Les?" my mother said brightly.

There was a pause on the tape, the sound of ice clinking against glass. "I got hit on the head," my father finally said. "By a rock."

"And Ernest saved you!" gushed the professor.

"No," my father said. "I died."

They all laughed on the tape, even the professor—once again, just a little bit after everybody else. When the laughter died down, Charlie egged my Dad on.

"But seriously, Les," Charlie said.

"Yes, very seriously," said my mother.

"I am serious," Daddy said. "As far as I could tell I was dead. The last thing I remember was the ground rushing up at my face, and a kind of funny feeling that the world was all very far away and not too interesting. And then—"

"Yes?" said the professor in a hushed voice.

"Nothing. Blank, black nothing. For a very long time, I guess."

In truth, I don't know how long I was lying there. When I came to, there was a buzzing in my ears and a low chattering among the rocks in the white haze before me. I tried hard to focus on what just seemed to be spots moving unaccountably. I couldn't. I felt around for my glasses, and found them—or found most of them, anyway. They were broken somewhere at my feet, and even if they weren't I would have been half blind with sweat and fear and the terrible glare of that East African sun. And that damned buzzing—what new menace would that turn out to be?

The buzzing sounded like insects, but not quite. And the spots were my assailants—hamadryas baboons, deadly cunning desert fiends. I saw the blurred image of a rock coming and ducked in time, and I heaved one back just as I dodged another, but a flat bit of shale got me in the knee. I bent to pick up more stones. I heard, rather than saw, the rocks that suddenly sent a searing, blinding sensation through my skull like I'd been hit through a heavy wet cloth thrown over my head. I simply felt the ground rise up again and thud against me. Now they could close in and make their aim really count. This time I was sure they would. I had to get up, go behind a rock of my own, find more rocks to defend myself. I pushed up with my good right arm, but nothing happened. Nothing? No, that wasn't right. Something, a small thing occurred just then. It was the buzzing. It grew louder.

Suddenly, I realized that the rain of deadly rocks had slacked off, and what I had taken to be buzzing was the sound of the jeep, our lovely vehicle, making it up the track behind the escarpment, in low gear.

It was Papa and the jeep. I tried to get up again. I wanted to see him—just to see him. I tried to push myself up, but the mechanics of it was beyond me. My arm pushed, but I didn't move even six inches. Instead, blood dripped off my face, making faint drops that the dust absorbed almost immediately.

The jeep engine died and I heard Papa shout, "Hey, Baron!" I tried to call back. All that came out was a kind of "Arrgh." I coughed up some slime and dust and spit it out. Then I made a big noise in my throat and tried to bring my head back around. And when I turned, I saw him running toward me with the rifle. He'd seen the camp. "Baron—what happened? Who did this to you?"

"Apes," I rasped out. "Look over there. You were just in time . . ." I keeled over again. Out cold, until sunset. And then, by God, that was a sunset. The most beautiful sunset I have ever seen. Not just because there is something about the desert air that makes the colors more vivid, and not just because this was a great sunset even for the desert. It was because I was there to see it, and a few hours before I would have bet heavily against that.

That night, over a second whiskey and with the campfire blazing with the blue-green flames from driftwood Papa had brought in the jeep, I told him what had taken place during those incredible four hours at camp out there on the Sudan escarpment.

Actually there had only been a fifteen-minute pitched battle when I knew that my training on the high school baseball team might be all I had between me and gooey death. I was pitching without a bullpen against a whole troop of baboons.

Papa kept yelling about how stupid I was to have insisted on staying there in the camp. He even said something about how stupid he was to have let me stay, and Papa could never admit that something might be his fault. It was stupid of me, but it was also getting a little tiresome, just the two of us in the jeep in that godforsaken desert. I thought it would be a fine break from the hunting if I stayed with the camp while he went to get the water.

"Wait a minute, wait a minute. You said you weren't actually hunting the baboons," the professor interrupted.

"No, of course not," Dad answered.

"King cobras," Willeford said quickly.

Followed just as quickly by Mom, with, "I thought it was tigers, Les."

"Both," Dad continued without missing a beat. Beside me, my husband snorted and my daughter gurgled with delight.

"But that's—in Africa?" the professor asked, incredulously.

"We were en route to a coastal village where we could

catch a ship to India. Papa had set up this hunt," my father told him. "Only we were hit by those baboon bandits. The little bastards were responsible for dumping out all our water supply. Nobody wastes water out in a desert, but we found our last two jerry cans of water opened, on their sides, and empty beside the jeep. We were only fifteen miles from the Red Sea and we had an evaporation outfit with a big Coleman stove to run it. With less than three gallons of gas, we could convert thirty gallons from the Red Sea into twenty gallons of fresh water in less than a day. But Papa knew of a well not too far off where he could fill the cans with fresh water we could boil. We'd have potable fluids in less time and without the brackish taste.

"I said I would stay and guard our gear and catch up on my own writing. Papa figured he would be back in three or four hours. We knew the break would do us both some good."

"What kind of writing were you working on?" the professor asked.

"I was keeping a journal back then. I wanted to get some of this trip down while it was happening. I was always amazed at the way Papa delivered one-liners—he did it so goddamned unexpectedly. Jesus, the guy would say fifteen or twenty wonderful things in a day. In passing or while the wind was blowing hard or while the jeep was blowing its horn he'd say something unbelievably good and you'd think: *Son of a bitch! If there was only some way to keep this stuff.* I just had a brief time in the evening when I could write, and I only got the two or three really best things he'd said sometimes. Sometimes I wouldn't."

"And you kept this journal the whole African trip?"

"Wouldn't you?"

"Did you keep—ah, do you still actually *have* the journal?"

"Oh, I expect it's around somewhere."

"I can't help but wonder about some of the things Ernest might have said—"

The professor trailed off, and there was a pause on the tape. Then I heard my father say, "Well, I guess it's getting late."

Another short pause, then the scrape of a chair and Charlie Willeford said, "All right, Les, thanks for the drinks."

"Please," the professor said. "I didn't mean—I beg your pardon, Les, truly—but you must know what a notebook like that could mean to scholars who—"

"Sure, scholarship is awfully damned important, isn't it?"

"I like to think it is."

"More important than good manners?"

"No, of course not, but—"

"I'm in the middle of a story here. I would like to get on with it."

There was a very short pause and then the professor said, "Please, Les, I would love to hear how the, ah, the baboon story comes out. If you would be willing."

"Without further interruption?" my father demanded.

"Absolutely," the professor answered.

My father grumbled a little and I heard a chair scrape. "Well, all right then," he finally said. "Where was I?"

"You were writing in your—*notebook*," the professor prompted him, and there was such naked lust in the way he said that one word that I snorted—and had the bizarre sensation of hearing my father make almost the exact same sound on the tape.

"That was it," Dad said. "My notebook. All right." He took a breath and once again launched back into the story, apparently without missing a beat.

So this was one of those moments when I sat there making notes, glancing up to watch the little desert quail go after the insects that buzzed around. I was under a canvas fly pitched on a taut rope between guyed poles, but it was the most pleasant place you could imagine with the breeze stirring. In the canvas chair at the small folding table, I could do my writing and look out over the surrounding country.

The great black buzzards, kites they call them, would come sailing slowly in from the coastal lowlands and catch the updrafts at the edge of the escarpment. Then they'd flap and rise some more and float around looking for lizards or carrion to eat. When the shadow of one would come sweeping in over the rocky brush piles, the quail would grow silent until it had disappeared. The kites must not have been too particular about what they ate, even in the feathered kingdom, for the quail did not trust them one bit.

It was just after one of these swift gliding shadows had crossed the area in front of our camp that the first incident occurred. I had been trying to figure out how those two water cans could have gotten from the back of the jeep and opened and dumped on their sides. It was spooky. There had been no unusual noises beyond the firelight the night before. And in the bright glare of midmorning, it all seemed fantastic. We'd surely have remembered if either of us had lifted them out of the jeep. And we would have carried them over to the cook tent.

Staring into space and thinking about this, I caught a movement off to one side. I turned and kept watching the spot for a couple of minutes and there was nothing more. The only sound was the happy buzzing of inquisitive flies that investigate everything in that arid land during the daylight hours. They always disappeared about dark, but right now they were everywhere.

I continued to wait and watch, and remembered that after a magnificent sunset the night before, there had been some distant barking that I took to be jackals. Four Nuer tribesmen we'd sign-talked with earlier in the week had made barking noises and pointed all around. We figured they were telling us that jackals were in the area.

While I watched the spot where I thought I had seen some movement, I studied the small blue doves taking dust baths in front of the scrub acacia this side of the first rock pile. They were having a grand time, occasionally flitting up into the branches to coo–coo and preen before settling down for the midday siesta here in the escarpment well above the valley of the dried-up Adakmana River. We were on the west side of the Jebel Chelhinde, not more than fifteen miles in a straight line from the Gulf of Aqiq, a little indentation on the west side of the Red Sea, just above the border with Eritrea. The railhead at Suakin lay some seventy miles north of us.

I had just given up watching and flipped open a writing pad when I caught movement again from the corner of my eye. It was . . . much closer. A damned big animal of some sort. And now I realized it had been moving in, stalking, slowly working closer under cover of those other rock piles.

I stood up. Immediately there was a strange chattering, a kind of cross between a jungle bird and Woody Woodpecker, a very creepy sound. Then I heard the first rock. I say heard because I was still back under the tent fly, unable to see the sky above me. It had been lobbed high and accurately. It slashed through the white canvas leaving a long gash and landed with a thud just beyond the table.

This was too much. I came out from under the sun shelter and had the misfortune to find I had been expected, as they say. A second stone smaller than the first was in the air before I stepped out. It caught me in the scalp as I stepped into the open. It was only a small blow but it hurt like hell and it was annoying to realize I had literally walked into a missile that could have been aimed at the tent. When I wiped at my forehead, there was a smear of blood on my hand.

I looked up, still more annoyed than worried. And there in the full heat of noon I saw what I was up against for the first time. There were two crouching forms peering out. As I watched, a third and then a fourth emerged from behind the rock pile to begin their attack on the camp itself. By the ruffs of long neck-hairs, I could see that they were hamadryas baboons.

To these desert inhabitants, I was just an object of curiosity, so far. I couldn't smell really dangerous to them, like a leopard could. We were harmless—we didn't even have a dog with us, but at that moment, I sure wished for one. I figured a few excited yelps from a coonhound might set these desert gangsters on their heels. But what the hell—they were only monkeys, right? "Harmless communal primates."

Almost without thinking, I reached down and picked up a rock. I was deciding which would be my first target when I stopped. For a moment I stood there frozen like some Greek statue. Then I quickly turned to the side of the tent and walked rapidly back to the rear. There was more brush there, and I badly needed cover.

I had seen that the rocks and the draw just west of our cleared space were absolutely alive with baboons. Hundreds of them. They were communal, all right, and it looked like they were communing after my blood. As I retreated I heard the rattle of stones landing on the tent and on the gear stored around the area I had just vacated.

I withdrew as strategically and hastily as a lone man could. To stand there would have been suicide and to try to beat them off with just my two arms would have been equally futile. Why? Why did I think that? They were just baboons, right?

Right—but in my swift survey, I had seen two of those four-foot-tall powerhouses wind up and throw. That's what they did. They wound up to throw a curveball overhand, just as we do out on the baseball diamond. They didn't act like bowlers-on-the-green. They took their time and threw overhand like Dizzy Dean, Bob Feller, and you and me. And they had control—that deadly accuracy could not have been accidental. And when I multiplied those two by the gang I saw lurking in the wash, I began to think it might add up to something pretty ugly.

Later when I was telling this story, I was assured that these rogues really are deadly. They have successfully attacked men and leopards many times, and stoned them to death with simple delight.

In this case I had the luck to cheat them of their victory. I used one of Hannibal's classic moves. First I withdrew—always a good idea when you're badly outnumbered. And then I found cover, and watched.

The things that took place next would hardly be given

credence by any academic or historian, but few men alive have ever seen hamadryas baboons in the wild, making free with a simple camp. It's an unbelievable sight, like watching the sack of Rome. It had everything: greed and looting, wild celebration, and even rape. The males satisfy their curiosity first and the females look for food. Then the males mount the females—not just once, but twice.

I'll tell you what, they loved our supply of Aunt Jemima pancake flour most. It lasted a good long time because it was in several small bags and each one was discovered as a separate triumph. From my lookout post behind the acacia shrubs, I saw them slowly going through the entire supply of Papa's favorite breakfast. They would sprinkle it all over each other and then lick it. Of course that turned their tongues to slurpy glue and soon their matted, dusty coats had taken on a gummy sheen and they were covered with spare provisions they could lick for days to come.

They got into everything, turned the whole camp into their trash heap. They opened every box, every sack, dumped everything onto the ground and danced in the ruins. Only our trunk locker defied them. The brass snap lock was too much for them. They pried at it, banged on it, jumped on it, picked it up and slammed it down like drunk draftees during the war, but they could not get it open. I remembered somebody in Key West had sent Papa a fruitcake and he had stuck it in there. The baboons may have smelled that, or maybe just hearing all the things thumping around inside was driving them wild with curiosity.

When I finally looked at my watch I realized I had been hiding in the scrub brush, peering through the shiny leaves and watching with fascination the complete destruction of our camp, for more than three hours. We had dealt with horned vipers, scorpions, and five blowouts in one day on this trip. But now I crouched there helpless, just watching—until they got my briefcase open.

All of a sudden, I just couldn't stand any more of it. I gathered a pile of rocks and stormed out from behind the bushes. There were at least fifty of them, maybe more, but I had the element of surprise with me—nobody had ever dared to just walk right toward a whole colony of them like that before, I'm sure. It was as though a man from Mars were visiting. There was no movement. They just stared, and then they began moving off.

And that was when I fell for their tactics. "Git! Shoo! Scram!" I yelled, waving my arms, and throwing a stone at the nearest one. It knocked dust in his lap and he got the idea. The whole bunch moved steadily away out to one side of the camp, but as they passed the first rock pile, they remembered they could throw, too.

Well, I was suckered completely out into the open when they suddenly stopped moving. That's when the rocks started singing in with deadly seriousness.

Now, I've never personally seen a man stoned to death, but I remembered my old Sunday-school lessons and it seemed incredible that this was happening to me, stoned to death without some Old Testament reason. One small difference—I never heard of anybody in the Old Testament throwing back, and I sure did. But I was badly outnumbered, and I could not have lasted much longer. I was down and almost out when Papa arrived.

"But why didn't you just stay hidden? You said you looked at your watch and it had been three hours. Didn't you realize he'd be back with the jeep soon?" the professor demanded.

"I was just so damned angry—when they got my briefcase open, they'd gotten my journal and they were licking the pages. That did it. Few things are sacred to a writer, but this . . ."

"So you lost all your work?"

"I didn't say that," Dad answered. "But it did make for interesting reading, between the bloodstains."

"What bloodstains?"

"When I collected my things later, I found the journal a hundred yards from camp, blood all over it. I thought perhaps I had hit one of the animals with a lucky rock, but after I found my briefcase I knew better."

"Why's that?"

"It seems that one of the baboons cut off a finger when the

metal lid slammed down on it. That finger was still there, inside the metal case. Papa suggested I dry it and hang it on a key chain."

"Did you?"

"Of course. By this time I had quite a collection. A croc's tooth, an ostrich spur, and a monkey's finger."

I SNAPPED OFF the tape player and turned to my husband and daughter. Pookie was asleep on the comforter. "Well," Jeff said. "This could be your proof."

I shook my head. "This is too weird."

"*Waaayy* too weird," Bear said. "Did Grandpa really carry that stuff around on a chain?"

I shook my head. "I remember my father carrying a tiger's claw in his wallet, forever. He said it was the Hemingstein good-luck charm."

"Heming*way,* not stein," Bear corrected.

"No, Hemingstein. It was a nickname Uncle Ernest invented for his family when he was in high school. Back then, it was fashionable to be anti-Semitic, but Ernest wasn't. And I think he wanted to make a statement."

"What's anti-sizmit?"

"It means to hate Jewish people," Jeff answered. "It's a kind of prejudice."

"Oh," Bear said. She knew that word. "Was Ernest prejudiced?" she asked.

"No," I answered. "He had lots of Jewish friends—writers, artists, and doctors. And remember you met Mr. Forbes, the black man in Key West who Uncle Ernest used to box with? He said Ernest was a true friend, and not prejudiced. Ernest hung out with all kinds of people in Cuba and Bimini, all over the world. He didn't care about race or any of that. All he cared about was if they were honest."

"So what happened to the Hemingstein good-luck charm?" Jeff asked.

"I don't know. I never saw it after Dad died."

Bear added, "Good. It sounds *sooo* gross."

"Well, I think it's pretty cool," Jeff said. "Kind of macho. You know: Don't mess with me, I've got a monkey's finger, man. And I know how to use it, too—so back off."

"Very funny, Daddy," Bear said with a straight face.

"Yeah, it is. Tell your friends," Jeff said, also straight-faced. He leaned over and put his finger on the Play button. "Maybe now your mom will find out where your grandpa got the tiger claw."

He pushed the button.

"So tell me, did you and Ernest ever make it to your big hunt?" the professor asked on the tape. "Ah—tigers, was it?"

"We did. And we bagged our tiger, too."

"What about the cobra?" Charlie Willeford butted in.

"And the cobra," my dad said. "We got them both. As far as that goes we were even more successful than we had hoped. But—" He paused on the tape and I could almost hear the professor leaning in.

"But what, Les?" the professor said. "Please, go on."

Dad sighed. "It never turns out well, even when it turns out the way you had planned," he said. "You always end up paying more than you can afford."

"You mean the native guides cheated you?" the professor asked.

"Listen," my dad said, sounding a little peeved. "You can't cheat somebody who doesn't let you cheat them. You think Papa would let anybody cheat him? Papa knew people—didn't you learn anything from all those books? No, the guides didn't cheat us. If there was any cheating going on it was on our part. We cheated death."

"Easy, Les," my mom said in the background, and Charlie laughed.

"All right," my dad said. "Maybe it sounds corny. But what my brother used to say was that if you haven't been there you can't know how it was. So I can tell you that we faced death, but what does that really mean to someone like you, Professor?" There was no answer, just a crackling sound from the old tape. "Well, it's true, corny or not. Not only did we face death, but death won."

A pause. The old tape crackled again.

"Excuse me?" the professor said at last.

"Death . . . won," my father said, slowly and carefully.

"Oh, but that's—I mean, you didn't— What happened?" the professor stammered.

"I'll tell you," my father said.

"NOBODY DIED, DID THEY?" Bear demanded. "What's he mean? Come on, Mom!" Her voice was a little too loud and Pookie woke with a frown and an unhappy gurgle. I picked up the baby and began to rock her.

"I don't know what he means," I told Bear, "I don't know this story."

"Hush!" Jeff said, waving us off. "We'll miss this if you two keep jabbering." He leaned closer to the player.

FIVE

I WAS IN A CAVE and I could hear the soft *pit, pit, pit* of the raindrops as they splashed on the ground outside, some twenty yards behind me. It was just an afternoon shower, but at a time like this, I concentrated on every little sound. I can remember a bird's call coming from far down the hill, and the clatter of wings past the cave's mouth.

Everything suddenly seemed so clear, sharp, and hard-edged. For ten yards ahead of me, there slowly arose an eerie whitish object six inches wide and nearly as tall as I was. At its upper end it swelled like a great spoon, three times the width below. And at the top of the swelling there were two tiny eyes that reflected the light from my flashlight. The object swayed slightly, and then I distinctly heard what I had been listening for.

Hsssss!!

King cobra.

My heart seemed to skip two, maybe three beats. And yet I stood there like I had grown roots, and just stared. Because in spite of the incredible danger, what I was watching was a truly majestic movement. It held its body erect by muscles strong enough to crush a full-grown ox, and was guided by a brain that must not have faced the challenge of being hunted by a man in years. And yet, there it was, reacting to me with perfect, deadly efficiency. The great snake began to advance, correcting its balance as it approached by slight changes in its column.

The undulations of the snake held me in absolute fascination. For a full moment I truly didn't think about the deadly situation I was in. I marveled at the skill, or sustained anger, that kept that great hood spread, and I tried to guess the snake's size.

Now, Papa and I are not small men. So when I found that the cobra was staring at me eye to eye, I knew this was a big snake. As the slightly weaving column of muscle and venom advanced, I mentally calculated the overall length of this moving death. It was reared up a good six feet. I knew that a king cobra could raise its body a bit more than one-third of its length. So this specimen must have been at least eighteen or twenty feet.

And when Papa had first spotted it, even he had declared it possibly the biggest poisonous snake in the world. . . .

That single word—*poisonous*—brought me back to reality.

Right there in the ancient cave in the Nilgiri Hills, at the edge of the largest unvisited plateau in southern India, I was face to face with the Lord Naga of a million legends and even more deaths. A truly great king cobra, who ever so calmly was coming out to see what right I had to disturb him on this Sunday afternoon.

Papa had hired a young Toda tribesman named Hadi to show us the way through the foothills of the Nilgiri plateau, but Hadi was on the way back to the railway station to bring the lunch we had left behind. And Papa had taken the left flank of the split tunnel, while I had taken the right in an effort not to lose this monster.

To show you what a fool I was, I had hoped for the luck of being the one to find this enormous creature and corner it.

My wishes were answered, but they were without luck.

The day had certainly begun with great promise. In tracking down this beast, I saw the walls of the cave reflecting tiny flashes of green from my flashlight. I chipped off some of the dark rock and found myself holding a beautiful piece of jade. I glanced ahead and saw an even larger piece jutting out. Well, it's no surprise that my mind was no longer on the hunt. I put down my gun and tried to loosen the fabulous chunk of rock, but it wouldn't budge. A wonderful find—and I had to wonder if there was more. I moved ahead, spotting more jade in the walls some twenty feet ahead of me. But then I also saw the figure of the snake. It was surprisingly close—a great deal closer than my gun, which was leaning against the cave wall twenty feet behind me.

I had just found a fortune in jade. But with that snake closing in on me I was sure I would never get out alive to enjoy it. Without my gun, how could I defend myself?

You don't have to tell me I had been stupid or shortsighted. I know it full well. But before you judge me too harshly, let me explain how we came to this place.

Papa had heard about the great tigers and snakes of this region and was determined to go. He pulled a lot of strings at the various embassies, and in just two weeks we were stepping off a merchant steamer onto a dock in Bombay. We quickly arranged passage by train to the Nilgiri Hills.

When we arrived at the train station, Papa called the stationmaster over. After a few questions he sent us to talk to an old Tamil man, one of the plains people. He spoke to us in soft, beautifully accented English. "There are many kinds of animals. You can hunt the tigers that kill cattle coming down the ravines. And the great snakes you will find in the dense growth outside our village."

Papa then asked him, "Is there anyone who knows where these tigers and snakes are?"

"You will need a Toda, not one of my people," the old man answered.

Now, the Toda are the people of the plateau and few came to this area. But as it turns out one Toda man named Hadi was there. And while Hadi spoke far less English than the older man, he agreed to take us on a hunt. We took very little with us. The light load made for easier crossing of the muddy paths that took us beyond the settlement and out to the wild foothills of the region. Besides the train at the station there were simply no vehicles to be had. This hunt was on foot.

Papa seemed to get along well with Hadi. There was no pretense to live up to, no legend of Papa the hunter. He was unknown in this land. I remember he joked about Hadi's long, dark, curly beard and brown turban, and how a turban could be attractive on a pretty woman. I think he truly meant for Ms. Pauline, but his comment did not sit well with young Hadi.

"Wait a minute, didn't Ernest wear a towel over his head while fishing in the Gulf Stream?" the professor interrupted.

"Yes, and it started after this trip," my father replied. "Fishing friends used to call him 'The Mahatma.' Then later we switched to 'Old Master.' Usually when he reverted to the role of dictator captain."

"That happened a lot?" Willeford asked.

"Well, after a long day in the sun, fishing and drinking, Papa said things that he never would have said sober."

"Like what?" the professor asked.

"A couple of times I remember him saying, 'Listen, if you object to what's going on, just say so, kid, and I'll kill you.' "

"Ernest said that?" Mom asked, sounding surprised.

"Maybe twice, when he'd been drinking, but next morning he followed up with, 'I know last night I was a little tight, and if I said anything that hurt your feelings I apologize. I'm awfully sorry, but sometimes I get to talking a little too loud.' This, by the way, is a big apology when you get it from Ernest Hemingway—big brother or not."

"But did he ever apologize for placing you in such terrible jeopardy?" the professor asked.

I heard my father snort. "What the hell does that mean?"

"Just that from what you're telling me these hunts seemed to put you more in harm's way than Ernest."

"You didn't have a little brother, did you, Professor?"

"Um—no, I am an only child."

"I wonder how I knew that," Daddy said.

"You're saying your brother risked your life out of sibling rivalry?"

"Oh, hell, do I have to spell it out? I'm saying Papa never put me in any danger I didn't go into willingly. I knew what I was doing. If Papa had coddled me, that would have been the greatest insult either one of us could think of."

"Really. Why is that?" the professor asked.

I heard the wonderful sound of my father's laugh on the tape, a sound that made me feel like a little girl again, and Bear, seeming to sense it, put her hand in mind.

"Papa believed that if you're any damned good at all, whatever happens to you is your own damn fault," my father said, and Bear squeezed my hand.

"So that's where you got that," she said to me.

"Hush," I said, squeezing her hand back.

"Of course, this didn't hold true for Ernesto," Daddy was saying, "but it held true for everyone else. I'm not kidding myself, I was not the skilled hunter he was. But I think Charlie Thompson was even better than Papa. Maybe that's why Papa liked having me around. I didn't try to compete against him. You realize when you get older that every human being has blind spots about himself. Papa did, too. He always needed to be the best. And he usually was. But not always. Hell, nobody ever is. Maybe the last man who could walk on water, but I never got to meet him."

"Of course," the professor agreed.

"So do you want me to finish this story or not?"

"Please."

"Well then?"

"Er—you were speaking of Mr. Hadai . . . ?"

"Hadi. His name was Hadi."

I heard my mother murmur, "Bravo," and then Dad was back into the story.

I was impressed with Hadi. His people raised cattle and he was in this area to rescue those that had strayed. That's why he knew the area so well. We started our hunt looking for tigers, but failed to find any tracks. So Hadi took us to where he had seen snakes large enough to take down his cattle. That's when we found the trail of a big one, wide enough to resemble a tire track. It was clearly fresh, so we followed it. It took us through low thick brush toward a hill.

As we began to ascend, we followed the bank of a little stream and we moved from heavy growth, the kind that leaves a musky odor of plants drinking up the last night's rain, to a drier soil with more rocks and boulders and an occasional small bush.

The snake's trail led us to a hillside cave. By now we were all very hungry so Papa sent Hadi to go fetch the rest of our provisions. We were to wait by the mouth of the cave, Hadi was very clear about that. I remember his deep brown eyes, deep-set below that turban, and his great black beard, as he used signs and his few English words, telling us not to go into the cave until he returned.

We said we wouldn't, and we meant it—but things don't always go the way they are planned. See, the great snake decided that it, too, was hungry—and Papa and I were just foolish enough to believe we couldn't possibly be on its dinner menu.

We were sitting with our backs to the cave and I was talking about the delightful things our food pack held—the fifth of Canadian Club, four tins of sardines, some English biscuits—when we suddenly heard the loud *hsssss*. It was the kind of moment when the hairs on your neck quite truly stand on end and your heart sinks to your kneecaps.

I remember Papa moving quickly, more like a soldier than a hunter. He grabbed his gun and rolled in one fluid motion, firing into the dark mouth of the cave. We saw movement and knew the snake had retreated.

You have to understand how it was. When Papa made up his mind to do a thing, no matter how dangerous, it was far easier to go along. And it was damned near impossible to think about questioning his authority at a moment like that.

I suppose, too, that I thought my fear could keep me alive. I knew it was a mistake to go into the cave. Call me superstitious, but a man should enter the earth only once, when he's dead. At my young age, I was in no hurry to join the ranks in Hades. But the hunt was on, with Papa leading the charge.

"Come on, Baron. Grab your gun and light!" he said, and there I was following him into that terrible dark hole.

Once inside, we had snake trails everywhere. It was clearly a prodigious serpent's den. Papa kept his light on the cave floor. We walked about ten yards in and found a point where the cavern split into two passageways. I paused and tried to see what was ahead down each branch, but it was darker than a coal miner's ass.

"Come on, Baron," Papa said. "Take the left, I'll take the right. Christ, I hope I can bag this beauty!"

And so Papa went one way and I went the other. In just a few moments we were separated as thoroughly as if we were on different planets.

That's when I found the snake. Or maybe I should say, the snake found me.

As I said, I got distracted by the jade. And then I heard that terrible hissing and looked up to see the monster.

Well, my flashlight was at my feet. It was heavy, unlike today's plastic things. I shined it at the great white moving snake and yelled for Papa. I knew he couldn't reach me in time. So I held completely still. All except for my hand holding the light; that shook, and I couldn't stop it.

Then I saw that the snake was following the spot of light. I moved it from side to side, then across the cave floor. The snake watched the light cross the floor. As it neared, the head of the beast swooped down and struck, leaving a fine line of venom on the dusty floor.

I'm pretty sure you've never seen a king cobra strike. Certainly not that close. You can't hope to imagine the speed of the thing, the total cold power and grace, as it slashed forward and made the rock ring like it had been struck with a hammer. I certainly didn't see it coming, and it scared the hell out of me. I jumped back.

That was my real mistake. I had moved. And that huge and deadly head came up and saw me.

Now the snake focused on me. Papa had told me that any big snake could strike a full third of its length, and with this great cobra's head almost level with mine, I knew I'd have to keep more than six feet between us.

I took a few steps back and the snake matched me. I could hear its breath in the cave's silence. I fully expected it to come racing at me and sink its fangs in. But I slowly crept backward. A few more steps and I could round the turn and run toward the cave's mouth. The snake followed, but made no move to attack. I was sure I was going to make it . . . until the heel of my left foot caught on a clump of rock sticking up from the floor.

I fell.

The great snake drew back in a coil to strike. Time stopped. I held my light on its huge head, helpless and spellbound. I knew this was it. I was about to die—but I knew how quick it would be, too, and some small part of me still admired the cold and deadly beauty of that perfect killing machine as it stretched above me, reared back, tensed to strike, and—

There was a loud *bang* and then a fleshy *splat*. For a moment I thought the sound was that great pile-driver of a head slamming me through the pearly gates. But then I opened my eyes and realized that I still held the flashlight in my hand, and it was no longer illuminating the snake's great head.

I moved the light down and saw the writhing mass on the cave's floor. And a moment later, while I was still too stunned to move, Papa knelt down beside me and whispered, "Thanks for giving me the kill, Baron. Christ, what a magnificent animal!" I guess after the croc, he felt I owed him.

But in truth, I would have to say I was very, very happy he killed that snake.

"What did he mean, 'Thanks for giving me the kill?' Did he really *need* so much to be around death?" the professor asked.

"Where the hell did that come from?" my father snorted.

"Ah, well, I know he was quoted as saying, 'if I don't kill animals, I'll kill myself.' "

"So you think he would have killed himself if I had shot the cobra? Is that it, Professor?"

"No, no, certainly not, I'm only postulating that, ah, there was some sort of dark need."

My mother laughed and I heard Charlie chuckling. "Interesting," Charlie said.

"A dark need to die?"

"No, that's not what I meant, not really—"

"Then what are you trying to say, Professor? To me, it's a pretty simple statement. I would think to any real man, it's pretty simple."

"Watch it, Les," my mother said. "I understand it, too."

Charlie laughed.

"I merely meant," the professor began carefully, "that your brother's obsession with killing things seems to have had a strong self-destructive component to it that seems, on the face of it, self-aware as well, and I wondered if you considered it *prima facie* evidence of an intuitive cognition of predestined self-destruction, or—"

"Jesus Christ," Charlie Willeford muttered, and my mother added, "Well, some of that's English, all right."

"All right, Herr Doktor," my father said in a patient and friendly tone. "I'll just tell you this. I've never known a person who really loved to kill people. I've known an awful lot of people who thought it a disgusting and disagreeable duty. Then again, I know certain literary professors who have proved very tempting. However, if you can confine your questions to the story, I'll consider it my *prima facie* duty to let you live."

This time the professor led the laughter, and when it had ebbed, he said, "You said you faced death and death won. What happened?"

"Oh," said my father, sounding for the first time like he'd been caught off-guard. "So you were listening after all, huh? Wasn't the king cobra enough for you?"

"Well, ah—is there more to this story?"

"You're the expert on stories," my father said. "What seems to be missing? On the intuitive cognitive level, I mean."

More laughter. Then I heard my mother clear her throat, an unmistakable sound even now. "What about the tiger?" she prodded.

"Yes, that's right," Charlie Willeford chimed in. "You were going to tell him about the tiger."

There was a long pause on the tape with a lot of throat-clearing. I looked between my daughters. Pookie was asleep again, but Bear looked at me full of questions. I didn't have any answers for her just then. I was still lost in the sound of my father's voice—and to be honest, I wanted to know about the tiger, too, just as much as Bear did. Jeff sensed it and patted my hand.

"What's happening, Dad?" Bear wanted to know. "Why are they all coughing and clearing their throats?"

"They're egging your grandpa on, and he has to come up with something good," Jeff told her. "Can't you hear it? They say something outrageous and he has to tell a story about it. It's turned into a game, a kind of top-this-if-you-can."

"I don't know," I said. "I thought so at first, but—"

"Of course," Jeffry insisted. "Listen to them. Your mom and Willeford are throwing out these ridiculous ideas and your dad has to go along with them, make it part of the story. We used to do the same thing when I was doing stand-up comedy.

My friends would heckle me with something totally nuts from the audience and I just had to go with it. God, your dad was good."

"Yeah, but he really did have a tiger's claw. How can it all be made up?" I asked.

"Hush," Bear said. "Grandpa is starting again."

SIX

WHEN HADI got back with our food, we worked the rest of the day to clean our prize snakeskin. I remember the underbelly scales were as big around as quarters. We must have taken two hundred pounds of meat off that beast. Hadi said it would feed his village for a week. For once it seemed we'd had luck. It seemed that way, but just for a while. Just until we headed back.

Hadi had led us down the hill and entered the dense brush at the bottom when he stopped suddenly and raised a hand to halt Papa and me. He stood there for a long moment, like a hunting dog on point, completely motionless, totally alert. And then he took a slow, incredibly careful half-step back.

That's when we heard it, too, just off the path up ahead. A low panting sound, then nothing. No sound at all—and then the most amazing explosion of bright color, motion, and muscle. And in that silence Hadi took the tiger's charge and died without making a sound. He had no time to call out or defend himself, and we had no time to react. All I saw was Hadi's brown arm flash upward and his turban fluttering to the ground. Then he was gone, and the silence returned, without Hadi or tiger anywhere to be seen.

Papa broke the silence. "Look out, Baron! There's another!"

I lifted my rifle to my cheek and fired; Papa fired, too. A second tiger leapt behind a ledge forty feet above us. There was a low rumble from where the first one had vanished. He had reappeared with Hadi's limp body in his jaws. Papa fired; I turned and shot, too, into the cloud of dust and spurting blood that was tiger and Hadi. Without waiting to see how effective our shots were, both Papa and I charged down the hill into the tall grass. We paused and reloaded.

Beyond us, the tiger on the hill called out for its mate, but the mate was lying in the dust, one paw twitching as the big cat stiffened into death. One of us had killed it, Papa or me, but it didn't seem all that important which. I was sick and disgusted. Papa seemed thoroughly ashamed; he had never before lost a man on a safari. The sweat was trickling down his cheeks and he looked like a man who had been deeply wounded.

I had a knot in my throat as big as an apple, and it hurt like hell. Hadi was more than just our tracker. In the short time I had known him, I believed we had become friends. Papa turned to me and asked if I could walk yet. I answered yes. He knew that aside from our father's suicide, I had never seen a dead man.

"You were there when your father committed suicide?" the professor broke in.

"Yes. I was thirteen. Home sick from school when I heard the gunshot."

"And you found your father's body?"

There was a long silence on the tape. I waited for my father to snarl, to put the professor in his place, to continue with the tiger story. But he didn't.

"I was a child," my father said at last. "I thought maybe he was still alive. He had locked himself in. So I lifted the pins off the door's hinges and found the body."

BEAR LOOKED HORRIFIED. This was the first she had heard of suicide in our family. I wasn't sure what to say, so I said nothing. I'm not sure I could have spoken anyway. I closed my eyes and felt my stomach clench into nausea. My mind fixed on the image of my own father's body lying on the red tile of the entryway in my childhood home.

I remembered the peaceful look on his face. It was like he was asleep, except for a red puddle under his ear and a small .22 pistol in his hand.

The tape continued, but the words were muffled to me. I looked over at my daughter. Jeff had an arm around her. She was upset, but more confused than anything else, and I knew she would be okay.

I was the one who needed healing.

The professor went on: "I have read that when Dos Passos was with your brother in Key West a package from your mother arrived. It contained a cake, some of your mother's paintings, and the gun your father had used. Dos Passos thought it cruel. As if she was saying, 'Here, Ernest, kill yourself, too.' "

"Christ, no," Dad said, and behind him I heard Charlie Willeford say, "Aw, for Christ's sake, that does it."

But Dad went on. "No, it's all right, Charlie. I can talk about it, and it's exactly the sort of crap that's been floating around for too long. Look, Professor. It's no secret that Ernest and Mother had their differences. But Ernest had asked for this gun. He told me I could have all the other guns, but that one was his." A short pause on the tape; the pitch of Daddy's voice dropped and he went on. "I went with Mother down to the Cook County courthouse. The gun had been seized by the coroner's office and we had to go through a certain amount of paperwork rigamarole to get it back. Mother honored Ernest's request and sent him the gun."

"Why did he want it?"

"What?"

"Why did he want that gun? It seems rather . . . morbid, don't you think?"

There was a long pause, filled only with tape hiss. Then my father spoke slowly. "I . . . think Ernest wanted to know . . . he wanted to make sure of where that gun was."

"Do you know what he did with it?" the professor asked.

"I believe he destroyed it. It never did show up again in any further doings with the family."

"What about the gun Ernest used?"

"Same thing. I understand one of his sons destroyed it right away. So it wouldn't be stolen for a memento. They took the damned thing out and rolled over it several times with a small truck. It was completely destroyed." There was silence on the tape, again leaving us listening to hisses and pops.

"The family exit—" my father said in a slow and heavy tone, and even over all the years in between, I felt the pain that was in those words. Abruptly, Daddy's voice changed, became brisk. "Look, we're here to talk about hunting. How about it?"

The professor cleared his throat. "Yes, of course. Please."

There was another long pause. I heard the clink of bottle against glass, and throat-clearing all around. Then, "Where was I?" my father asked.

"Surrounded by tigers," my mother said.

JEFFRY NUDGED ME. "See what I mean?" he asked. "They're feeding him straight lines—'surrounded by tigers'?" He squeezed my hand. "This really is great!"

I forced a smile. But it was hard for me to get back into the spirit of the tiger hunt. I was battling with a different beast. I had never really understood what my father had gone through with his father and then again with his brother. And then later, after all that, he had chosen the same way for himself. The family exit. He made it sound so noble.

But guilt and anger are the inheritance that suicide leaves, and they had been passed down to each generation. It had come full-strength to me, and I realized for the first time how truly it had marked me.

I looked over at my daughter and made a silent promise. It would end here, with this tape, and with my new understanding of my family's legacy.

And now the tape was more than just a collection of hunting stories. It was my journey of discovery, a way to understand my own past. And it was an important starting point for a thought I now realized I'd been fighting for almost fifteen years. I'd pushed it away and hidden it under a thick layer of carefully controlled emotions.

I'd never been able to understand why my father chose the family exit. I had fought off the thought that it was cowardly—Daddy was not capable of cowardice. And yet I had never been able to understand what he had done. But if these hunting stories were true, Daddy had shown the world his bravery. Was it fair to hope, to wish, to *need* these stories to be true? Maybe that said more about me than my father—but I began to believe for the first time something I'd pretended not to think about ever since I'd seen his body.

My father was not a coward.

Jeff whispered, "Hey, are you listening? You're about to find out about the lucky tiger's claw."

"Yeah," I said, and gave him a smile I really felt. "Now I'm listening."

Ernest was the first to get up. He walked over to Hadi's body and closed his eyes. The cat had snapped Hadi's neck and ripped his side out, leaving flesh dangling over his chest. I remember the way Papa touched the blood then looked up and said aloud, "God, you've taken a fine man. Please let me kill the other tiger."

He looked down at the blood on his hand for a moment. Then he walked back to me and sat down. "You all right, Baron?" he asked.

"I'm fine," I answered. "Are we really going after that other tiger?"

Papa nodded.

"Are you sure there's only the one?" I asked, and he laughed, just a little, but I could already see the eagerness coming back to his face.

"Just one," he said, and stood up. "But the light is getting lousy and we're still a long way from the village, so we have to hurry. And I want first shot, do you understand?"

I did understand. That's the way he was—it wasn't macho glory, either. He never did give a crap for all that. But he had standards. He knew absolutely what was right and what was wrong. And he wanted to settle with both tigers for Hadi's death. It had happened when *he* was in charge, do you see? So he felt responsible. And when he asked me if I understood, I did. I knew exactly what he was saying. As I've said before, he didn't apologize much, but he always tried to make things right again, as much as that is ever possible in this lousy world.

So Papa handed me my gun and we headed back up the

hill. Halfway up we heard a swelling roar that echoed through the trees and stopped us clean in our tracks. With the sun setting, there was a mist rising up over the vegetation. Visibility was failing fast.

"Stay close," Papa told me.

SEVEN

NEAR THE CREST we came out into a clearing and stopped dead. Straight ahead on the far side of the clearing we saw the big cat under a tree. Papa began a slow and careful approach and I stayed right beside him. The tiger watched us, its heavy tail thrashing back and forth spastically.

As we approached Papa whispered to me without taking his eyes off the cat. "It's the male," he said.

The tiger remained upright, his black-and-gold stripes showing clearly against the lush green foliage. When we were thirty yards away he stopped wagging his tail. His shoulder muscles bunched up and suddenly the cat bounded up and away from us.

Papa's rifle came up and went *crack* before I could even register the cat's movement. The shot entered the tiger's body along the rump. "Good," I shouted.

"Bad." Ernest hissed. "Christ, what a lousy shot. It wasn't clean."

"Whack him again," I said. But the tiger had already rolled into the tall grass and crawled into hiding.

"We'll have to follow him in there, Baron," he said. "We can't leave him wounded."

I wanted to say, "Sure we can." I knew very well, and so did Ernest, that there is nothing on this earth more dangerous than following a wounded predator into the tall grass. But I also knew as well as my brother that we had to do it. If you wound the animal, it is your sacred duty to finish it off, to end its suffering. Don't shoot something if you can't finish it off decently. That's the way we both were raised, and he didn't have to say anything more to me. "Right," I said, and I followed him into the grass. Mind you I was scared pea-green. But I didn't want Papa to go after a wounded tiger alone, and it had to be done.

"Here," he said, stopping and stooping low. I followed his finger and saw where the tiger had slipped through the grass on his belly and made it back into the jungle. The grass was broken, as if the cat had crawled part way, and there were streaks of blood along the right side of the track.

"He can't get far bleeding like that," I said, but Papa just looked at me and shook his head.

"I hope not," was all he said.

We tracked the animal's bloody trail for another hour, and by then the sun had set and we were in the dark. And just when we were both ready to call it off as entirely too risky and wait until morning, we heard the tiger's unmistakable call. It was a soft coughing sound, hard to describe but impossible to forget once you've heard it. You hear that sound and before you even realize what you're doing, you find yourself crouching with a dry mouth and a pounding heart.

I pointed left, meaning shoot left, and Papa nodded. He wanted to get close enough to make one shot count. We moved forward a few more steps and then Papa held out an arm to stop me. He nodded forward and I looked.

The tiger was there, up on a ledge, less than twenty feet away. It must have heard us because it coughed again and then roared. This time it was deafening. "I'll go first," Papa said. "He won't come out unless we flush him."

We both hit the top of the ledge at the same time. Papa moved to the left. I looked at the tiger, only half-visible in the gloom. The little light there was gleamed off his fangs as he roared again, but this time the ledge shook. I saw a vague movement but couldn't duck fast enough as the blur of the big cat came straight past me toward Papa. I heard Papa's gun *bang* twice and then the tiger crashed down the slope to the bottom of the hill.

"Christ, what a great beast! I'm sorry I had to kill him," Papa said, coming back for me. "He was just over you when I shot."

"I know," I answered, knocking the dust off my clothes. "That was excellent shooting. Hadi would have approved."

We walked back to the base of the hill as the moon finally rose into the sky. We came to where the great cat lay, so still and yet so fierce-looking, his huge teeth exposed by death. For a long moment we just looked down at the cat. He had tried to kill us, and we had killed him first, so you might think we would be relieved that we had won, or glad to see that tiger dead. But I know that I felt very fond of that man-killing beast, and I could see that Papa did, too. If you have never hunted you might not understand, but we just looked down at that tiger for a good long time.

"Would you like to keep any part of this wonderful beast?" Papa finally asked me.

"I don't think so," I said. "I want to remember him like this."

Papa looked at me for a long moment, and then looked back at the tiger.

We buried the cat in a shallow pit there at the foot of the hill. It took quite a large hole. That tiger was the size of a small horse. We didn't have any proper digging tool with us, but we kept at it until it was done.

When we finally made it back to Hadi and the other dead

tiger the sun was coming up. We dug another shallow pit and shoved the tiger in. Then Papa dug a grave for Hadi and I collected some big rocks to roll on top of the grave to keep the scavengers away. When I was done, I stood and looked down at Hadi's body. He seemed much smaller now. I picked up his turban, and something fell out and plopped at my feet. I bent over and picked it up.

A dried tiger's claw had been tucked into the linen. I stuck it in my rucksack and placed the turban beside Hadi. We filled in the grave and put the mound of rocks over it after saying a few words.

There was a long, hissing gap on the tape.

"That was the end of your hunt?" the professor asked.

"Yes, and then we had another two weeks to get back to East Africa."

"Did anything eventful happen along the way?"

"Haven't you learned anything yet, Professor? Traveling with Papa was the adventure. Everything happened. That's why you're here today. Things happened around Papa. People are still drawn to Papa."

Willeford laughed. "So stop interrupting the stories," he said.

"Of course," the professor said. "Please go on."

THE TAPE CRACKLED EXPLOSIVELY and thumped to a stop.

Before I could move, my daughter hit the Eject button. "Let's hear the other side," she said.

I said nothing and Jeff looked at me, one eyebrow raised. "Are you all right, sweetheart?" he asked.

"I'm fine," I said. I reached over and picked up Miss Pookie. There's something healing about holding a baby. Maybe it's the smell of their heads, the softness of their skin, or the cheerfulness in their eyes. Whatever it is, it fills the soul with hope, and that's what I needed.

"Then shall we hear some more?" Jeff asked.

"Come on, Mom," Bear urged me. "I want to hear the other side of the tape."

"Just a second, Bear," Jeff said, and he turned to me. "Honey—we can always put it off for a while."

"No!" Bear protested.

"I'm okay," I said. "Really."

He looked at me for a good long time as Bear fidgeted beside us. "All right," Jeffry said at last. "If you're sure."

I mustered a smile. "I'm sure," I said. "Let it roll."

"Yahoo," Bear said as she reversed the tape and slammed it back in. And then the second side of the tape hissed and popped and once more Daddy's voice filled the room.

EIGHT

Papa and I made good time crossing back into East Africa. But when we were traveling through Somaliland, we discovered a white safari gone bad. The party had run out of gas for their truck. To run out of gas is very bad and shows that you don't know what you're doing. And that usually means worse things are about to happen. This time was no different. These hunters were about to become the hunted.

My first clue that something was wrong was when a lone woman waved us down. That should have been enough to signal big trouble—because she was beautiful, and on safari a beautiful woman always means trouble.

She stood on top of a rock cliff maybe twenty feet high. She wore a sheer white dress that clung to her small frame and rippled about her in the hot wind. From a distance, with the heat distorting the air between us, I was sure she was a mirage. A little closer and we would see that she was nothing more than a stunted tree, with a rag on it whipping in the wind. After all, how could there be a lone white woman here, especially one so seductively beautiful?

But we got closer and she was no mirage. She was a lovely, slim woman, and although we could tell she was in trouble of some kind, she looked awfully good standing up there on that rock.

"Do you see it too?" I asked Papa.

He grinned. "I sure do," he said. I knew he had been missing Pauline. It clearly cheered him no end to see such a lovely vision. And when we were sure that she would not disappear as we got closer, Papa really began to smile. She stood there on that rock in the middle of the plains like a beacon calling to us.

We left our jeep and approached. She turned and called over her shoulder, "Come see what I've done. We're saved."

We hiked up through the boulders toward her, like sailors to a Siren. I remember she had the most wonderful smile, and the perfect white teeth and flawless skin of a well-kept woman. "My darlings, you're just in time. We've been without petrol for three days."

Papa gave me a look, then asked, "What kind of hunter leads his party out here without the fuel to get home?"

"Oh, Johnson had it all set up. A native trader was to come with fuel each evening. Only he hasn't been here in three days." She lowered her voice. "I think the man's dead."

"More likely dead drunk," Papa said, laughing.

We heard the men's voices coming from under the wide-topped acacia trees that shaded the canvas camp below. I counted four men: two native guides, the white hunter, and this woman's husband, who was climbing up to meet us. He walked with a limp and used a walking stick.

"I'm Dr. Greg Brown," he said, holding out his hand to greet us. Brown was a stocky, bald man in his forties with a battered nose. Clearly he had entered too many fights, and lost most of them. Strange for a doctor, but perhaps not for a man with such a beautiful wife. His face was red from the climb, and he glanced nervously at Papa. "I see you've met Lori."

"Well, not officially." Papa smiled and held out his hand. "Like a flower from home, waving in the sun." He kissed Lori's hand and caught a jealous gleam from her husband's eye. "Perhaps it wasn't wise for you to come on such an adventure."

"Why?" Lori protested.

"Men in the wild are an evil lot, daughter," Papa laughed. "Men everywhere, for that matter."

"Agreed," Brown said. "And I've had my fill of this particular paradise."

Papa and I introduced ourselves. Dr. Brown and his attractive wife were impressed with Papa. Lori had even read one of his books—or so she said, but then she lacked any ability to talk about it, despite Papa's questions. He always had to pry when somebody said they liked his work. He couldn't just say, "Thanks," and let it go. He had to know why.

I don't know what he expected to learn from Lori, but he was disappointed. Still, she was an attractive woman and we had been out in the bush an awfully long time. So the two of them sat together while everyone else packed up the camp. I have to admit she was easy on the eyes, and she seemed nice enough, at first. Like most women, she hung on Papa. But after a few drinks, she started in on the good doctor.

Now, I know people talk when they're drunk. They say things drunk that they wouldn't say sober. They're not necessarily true things; people just say hostile, malevolent garbage because they think it's funny, or because of whatever demon there might be in drink. They say things they know will hurt the other person and in the morning they don't remember and can't understand why the locks are changed on the door.

In this case, Papa heard about Dr. Brown and his lion. He heard about it from the wife, in a voice that cut like a razor.

How Brown had run from the animal's charge, the worst thing a man can do on a hunt. Then to add injury to insult, Brown had fallen in his run and shot the end of his boot off. Lori told it very well. She pointed to him at the end, so we could see that his foot was bandaged pretty good, and said that clearly he was a better doctor than a hunter—or a man.

"Wait a minute, he shot himself?" the professor interrupted. "But I thought from the start of this—I mean, for a moment it seemed like it might be the couple from 'The Short Happy Life of Francis Macomber.' "

"Oh, I don't know. I think you're trying to read too much into this," my dad said. He gave a short laugh. "But—who knows?"

"Well, but it could—I mean, did this woman kill her husband?" the professor asked.

"No, haven't you been listening? If she had just hauled off and shot him, that would have been more humane. But as it happened on our trip—it was the white hunter who died."

"You're joking," the professor blurted.

"No, and it wasn't poor old Doc that did him in. Though he had every reason. His wife did have an affair with the man. That beauty took real delight in retelling it. Poor Doc, he had been sufficiently humiliated by his fear, hobbled by his own gun, and then taken apart by his wife the way only a woman can do it. And no one cared. He'd lost face. Hell, the whole camp saw him run. His wife was embarrassed, and when a man loses face with his wife, there's no gaining it back. Her affair with the hunter was just collecting another man's trophy."

"So what did kill the white hunter?"

Willeford answered, "Wild dogs."

"Oh, come on, dogs?" The professor chuckled.

"Not just any dogs, man. The cannibal dogs of El Kamir," Dad said with a serious tone. "Hundreds of hellhounds. Unimaginably fierce, traveling in great, vicious, hungry packs. From the moment I saw them, I knew someone was going to die."

"Seriously?" said the professor.

"Take a Rottweiler. Raise it in the wild in a hostile environment, where only the most vicious survive at all. Now multiply by a hundred fifty," Dad said.

"My God," the professor gasped. "Go on."

Well, by the time the camp was packed, it was late afternoon. Now you should know that in East Africa the dusk fades swiftly into night. And it's best not to be out at night—you want to be behind a *boma* with a good fire burning. But in this case, our goal was to get the camp packed and our spare fuel siphoned, and to caravan together to the town of Mogadishu. It was a sound plan, based on a lot of experience and plenty of smarts, and it should have worked. It would have worked, if the dogs hadn't mucked things up.

Papa, Lori, Doc, and I were up on the hill, looking around and trying to stay out of the way. The white hunter and his guides were stowing the gear below. We had just settled into a kind of awkward silence when the first gray-black head peeked from around a rock. It was a large head with pointed ears, and it was followed by a stocky, muscular body. The dog moved quietly toward the truck. Its short tail didn't wag, it just stuck straight up as the monster approached.

I said, "Do you see the dog?"

"What dog?" Papa asked, but before we could blink there were suddenly dozens of dogs coming out of the high grass and moving in on the men in the truck.

"Sweet Jesus," Papa said, and pushed Doc and his wife down. I crouched and moved to look over the edge, but Papa laid a hand on my back. "There's nothing we can do without guns, Baron. And if they hear us or smell us—we're dead."

There was a yell in Swahili. And we watched helplessly as the dogs boiled through camp. Both of the guides scrambled to the canvas roof of the truck. I think the oddest thing was that the dogs didn't even bark. They just kept moving forward with permanent snarls on their blunt ugly faces.

"Surely they'll eat our food and leave," Doc whispered.

"Nope, they won't eat anything, unless it's a fresh kill," Papa answered. And I think Doc realized what Papa meant by "fresh kill." Because just then two big males jumped up into the back of the truck, and a moment later the canvas above the truck's cab ripped open. One of the two guides fell into the truck's cab. He let out a loud scream that was cut off quickly as the animals were on him.

The surviving guide cursed at the dogs in Swahili. But moments later, we saw him scrabble back to the edge of the canvas and hunker down, scared, silent, and all we could hear was the sound of bones crunching from inside the cab.

The commotion brought Johnson from his tent. He had not seen the dogs and did not have his gun—not that any gun he might have had would have done him a lot of good against all those killers. So he just stood there. The moment seemed frozen. I still remember the face of the guide watching from the top of the truck, and Johnson's eyes. I'll never forget his eyes. He didn't blink. He just stared, like he could make those hounds back away with just his eyes.

No one moved—it seemed like forever. Then Johnson made a mad dash toward the closest tree. He had only twenty feet to cross, but the whole pack poured toward a spot just ahead of him. Johnson went down like a water boy tackled by two football teams. There was snarling, snapping, and finally one horrible gurgling scream. Johnson's throat was ripped out and in a matter of minutes his body was pulled apart.

By now we were all back on our feet, hoping to slip away while the dogs were busy. But as we stood, Lori saw what the hounds were doing to Johnson's body, and she screamed. Papa put his hand over her mouth, but it was too late. Her wail had been plenty loud enough, and below us we could see the dogs pause and perk up their ears. Then all those ugly gray heads began to swivel toward us.

"My God, look what you've done," her husband yelled.

"Me?" Lori returned. "You're the one that had to take this goddamned awful trip."

The good doctor grabbed his wife. "I should kill you."

"Knock it off," Papa bellowed, and shoved the doctor back on his sore foot. Brown dropped his walking stick and fell back on his butt. It was a strange moment, because instead of looking at the man, Papa focused on the falling walking stick as it rolled and fell to the rocks below. "That's it. Baron, we have to get that stick."

The pack watched us and grew tense. Two of the dogs were slouching their way up the slope toward us. But I didn't question Papa. If he had a plan, well, he was way ahead of the rest of us. I just kept my eyes on the dogs and went down on my stomach. Papa held my ankles and I dangled myself over the edge. The rock pushed hard against my chest and I stretched until it hurt, but I couldn't grab the stick; my fingers just brushed it, so close below me, and just out of reach. "Just a little farther," I gasped. I tried to wiggle and stretch—and as I did Papa's grip slipped.

Under me there were about fifty of the hungry brutes, and if I slid down there I would be dinner quicker than Papa could say "Oops." But I felt his hands tighten on my ankles, and I didn't slide any farther; just enough to reach the stick.

I closed my fingers around it. I had it. Papa pulled me up just as a big male dog came snapping at my arm. I took one good swing and connected with the monster's shoulder. He yipped and fell back.

"Out of the ballpark, Baron. You've bought us a few minutes."

"First time I ever tried to bat upside down," I said.

Papa chucked me on the shoulder and hefted the stick like a spear. "This could work."

"Glad to hear it. There are two hundred dogs down there betting against us."

"Do you feel that?" Papa asked, then wet a finger and held it in the breeze. "The wind. It's strong enough to make a grass fire. And it's blowing toward the plateau. With any luck at all we can drive these man-eating bastards back and make a run for our jeep."

"Fine, but don't overlook that we might be roasted, too," Doc Brown complained.

Papa might have said something pretty rough to him, probably would have at another time, or with a man he hadn't seen so thoroughly de-balled. Instead, he spoke to him like he would to a child. I think I was the only one there who knew what a huge insult that was.

"No," Papa began, "the grass will burn quickly and it

shouldn't take more than a minute for the flames to pass straight through camp. Then all that's left is hot, cindery stubble. Even with your bad foot you can get through that."

"Do I have a choice?" he asked. But Papa had already turned away. Doc Brown looked at me and licked his lips. I could see he was plenty nervous. But hell, we were unarmed and surrounded by a horde of savage, man-eating hounds, and they were closing in on us. We were all nervous. Papa and I were just better at hiding it.

"Relax," I told Brown. "When Papa gets a plan it's best just to agree with him. He's usually right."

"What about when he's not?" Doc asked me.

Before I could answer, we heard a soft exclamation followed by a shriek, and we both turned. Papa had ripped away the lower half of Lori's dress. "Easy, daughter, it's your life we're saving. Baron—your matches."

I watched as Papa twisted the cotton material around the stick, making a large Q-Tip. I struck the first match, but the wind blew it out. I cupped the second match in my hands and touched it to the material. It took a moment, but then fire spread across the cloth.

"Here, Baron," Papa said and gave me the flaming spear. "Make it good."

Now I have to tell you, I won a javelin toss back in high school, so Papa had a reason for letting me have this hero's moment.

"Which way?" I asked, looking over the camp.

"Right over there." Papa pointed to a grassy spot between our rocky ledge and the jeep. I nodded. It was a tough throw, what with the wind and the tension, but I took a breath and let fly. My flaming swab flew straight and true, arcing some thirty yards through the air. It hit the ground right where I had aimed. "Good one, Baron," Papa said. "Now let's hope she catches."

I did hope. I hoped like hell. If it didn't catch, we were going to be devoured by a pack of hellhounds. But as we held our breath and watched, flames began to lick the ground, and white smoke rose across the field as the fire spread. Once the scrub and the grass began to burn it spread faster than you can imagine. No fire before or since has ever looked so good to me.

Everyone cheered as that crackling orange line marched through the camp. The first dog saw it and started to back away, growling. Then a cinder crackled across the clearing and landed on one of the dogs working on Johnson. He yelped and chased around in a circle. The other hounds looked up and saw the fire and began to back away out of its path.

"Now!" said Papa. "Let's go!"

The dogs were backed up on the far side of the fire, but they watched us as we moved down the rocks and jumped to the burnt ground.

The thick smoke choked us, but we coughed and pounded each other on the back and loved it. We ran across the smoldering stubble toward our jeep. Our canvas top had caught fire and burned away, but that was the only damage. We got in and gunned it over to the safari's truck. The surviving guide had successfully moved it through the thick smoke. There was nothing much left of Johnson or the other guide.

Papa told the doctor and his wife that the foreign officials would be out in the morning and they should leave everything alone, just as it was. I think they were just as glad, considering the condition of the bodies. I was pleased to see that a couple of the dogs had succumbed to the smoke. We needed their carcasses as final evidence in the grisly killings.

BEAR CLICKED OFF the tape recorder and looked up at me with a pout. "You mean the dogs *died*?" she asked.

"Hey," Jeffry told her. "These aren't cute fuzzy puppy dogs. They just *ate* a couple of guys."

"But they didn't have to die," Bear said, still pouting.

"Yes, but honey," I said. "If the dogs hadn't died your grandfather and great-uncle might have been held for murder. This way what was in the dogs' stomachs could prove they were the killers."

"If this happened at all," my husband said. "It still sounds pretty wacky. Wild man-eating dogs? Come on."

"We could probably check it out," I said, and Bear's face lit up.

"Yeah," she said. "I'll go turn on the Discovery Channel!"

I laughed, and my husband did, too. "That would be the most fun way," I said. "But it might take a while before the right show came on."

"You know," Jeffry said, "I still have my shot-put ribbons from state meets. If your dad won a medal, I bet he would have kept it, too."

"Can we look, Mommy? I know it's there," Bear said.

"Where?" I asked her.

"In Grandpa's room," she said smugly. Jeffry started to laugh. It was one of our family jokes. We had stored about a dozen boxes of Dad's stuff in a closet under our stairs, and had started to call the closet Grandpa's room. It was virtually un-touched since we'd moved in. Mom hadn't been able to bring herself to go through the stuff after his death, and my sister and I had been told to leave it alone. Now after all these years, it almost felt like sacrilege. But I wanted to find answers, and looking through Dad's stuff seemed like the best place to find them.

"I'll put Pookie in the crib, if you get a flashlight," I said to Jeff.

"Meet you at the closet," he answered.

"Oh, boy!" Bear said. "We could find all kinds of stuff in there! Baboon fingers and tiger claws—and maybe there's some jade!"

"Well, there's definitely spiders, anyway," said Jeffry. "And a lot of dust."

I tucked Pookie into her crib. She slept on, with a sweet smile on her face. I met Jeff and Bear in the hallway by the closet. "You open it, Mom," Bear said. "It's your dad's room."

As I opened the closet door, I warned Bear and Jeffry, "Don't throw anything away unless we go through it first."

"You've got to be kidding," Jeff answered. He shined the flashlight on a stack of boxes. "It's worse than I remembered." They really were in bad shape. Only the movers had touched them since Dad's death. And while I'd love to say their bad condition was the movers' fault, in truth it was from the nearly two decades that the boxes had sat in Mom's dusty garage, through flooding, heat, humidity, and cockroaches. They were dirty, battered, torn—and a little bit creepy. Bear lifted the lid on one box and pulled out a clump of Kleenex.

"You really want to go through this wad of tissue?" Bear asked, making a face.

"Especially that wad of tissue. Mom never found the missing emeralds from Dad's South American trip. All I know is that Dad packed them in tissue."

"What a great way to hide them," Jeff said.

"Hey, it worked. They're still hidden," I pointed out.

"Jimmy Hoffa could be hidden in here," Jeff said. "Along with Judge Crater and Elvis. Isn't it in some kind of order?"

"No. Mom packed everything thinking someday she'd sort through it. But she never did."

"I think I hear something chewing back there," Jeffry said, pointing his flashlight at the bottom box in a stack of three.

"Probably cockroaches," I guessed.

"Gee, I hope so," Jeff answered.

"Maybe we should wait until morning, Mom," Bear added.

"Absolutely," Jeff agreed. "I'll just use a few cans of bug spray tonight."

"Okay. Get your hair and teeth brushed, and change into a nightshirt." I kissed the top of Bear's forehead. "We'll be in in a few minutes."

JEFF AND I TUCKED T. L. Bear into bed. We kissed her goodnight, and I was still kneeling at her bedside when she whispered, "I really do like your daddy. He was so brave."

"Yeah, he was. He faced almost everything, and usually came out on top."

"Only usually?" Bear asked me, and in her innocent question there were sharp edges that only I could feel. But I smiled anyway.

"I love you, darling," I told her. "Now get some sleep." I kissed her cheek and turned off the light.

It had been an extraordinary afternoon and evening, and I felt lucky and moved to have shared the discovery with my family, and to have introduced my daughter to my father. Yet I had not been able to relax and hear my father's adventures with simple enjoyment, the way my daughter and my husband so obviously had. Yes, they were great stories, and Daddy was a wonderful storyteller. Hearing his voice had brought back a flood of memories of the way he had held people spellbound when he wanted to spin a yarn.

But that wasn't the only thing I remembered. I still could not shake that one picture of my father. Funny how the mind freezes moments in time.

As I lay in bed trying to sleep that night, I remembered the last time I saw Daddy. The blood that pooled around his body was the same color as the red tile floor. Maybe it was not as ugly a scene as when he had found his father or, for that matter, the mess Ernest had left using a shotgun. But he was my father, and he'd been through the same ordeal himself, and he should have known. He should have known how painful it would be for his wife, for his children.

I remembered the look on my mother's face when she saw I was home. I had been in classes at the University of Miami and had stopped in at my dorm room to grab a bite of lunch. The phone rang. My roommate answered it, thinking it was for her—but it wasn't. I recognized the voice before he said his name. His words were simple. "I sold your dad a gun." He had more to say, but I only half listened beyond that first sentence. I repeated it a couple of times on the quick drive home.

There was no mystery as to why my father had bought the gun. At least it was clear to me. The only question I had was whether I could stop him. I played out a dozen heroic scenarios, always saving him just in time. It never occurred to me that it was too late.

"How did you know?" Mom asked. She had not called me, or my sister or brothers yet, and had been too busy dealing with detectives to stop me from entering the house. So there I stood in the hallway looking down at Daddy, and watching men in lab coats photograph his lifeless body.

"How did you know?" she asked again.

"Jack called," I answered, not looking away from Daddy. Was this an out-of-body experience? I was there, but I wasn't. It was like floating through an ugly dream.

"Who?" a bald detective barked.

"Jack, the guy who sold him the gun," I said, and turned to make eye contact with my mom. "He said Dad drove over to the repair shop and told him he needed a gun for security. Ten minutes later, Jack remembered I'd told him about Dad being depressed and the upcoming surgeries."

"I'll need to talk to this Jack. Where can I find him?" The detective made a note in his book.

"He's on Fifth Street. Jack's Foreign Car Care."

"He's a mechanic and Les's friend. He does a lot of work on Hilary's VW. He didn't know," I heard my mom say. "I asked Hilary to take the family guns out of the house three weeks ago. She left them with a neighbor, Dr. Howard Engle. That was just before Les's last surgery."

"What was he in for?" the detective asked.

My mother explained that my father had Type II diabetes. In the final stage, the arteries and veins collapse, so the surgery was to remove the damaged ones and replace them with plastic. My father called it better living by Du Pont. But if the surgery failed, he faced double amputation.

"You have to understand the kind of man Les was," my mother told the detective. "He wanted a life worth living."

I looked at my father again. *What were you thinking? Did you leave us a note? You had it under control—why did you do this?*

I stared at his body, but there were no answers. He seemed to be at peace; there was no contorted death mask. He wore only his boxer shorts. His pale legs stretched out across the tile in a natural position. He could have been asleep.

Did you shoot yourself lying down? What made you choose today, September 13? You hated the number 13. Did you just wake up saying, "today is a good day to die"? Or did something snap and you wanted to off yourself?

The only hint of his troubles was the two bright pink scars running from his groin to his feet.

Just three weeks earlier, he had helped me pack up my VW bug with everything I needed to start my junior year at UM. Although the university was only fifteen minutes away, I had chosen to live on campus. Dad stood in the driveway next to my car, clasped his hands together, and raised them in a wide circle like a victorious boxer.

"Hillsides, don't let anything get you down. I'm going to beat this. You watch." He stomped his feet and added, "Next time you come home, we'll get out on the water. I love you, daughter."

Lying in bed so many years later I could still hear his voice as clearly as I had just heard him on the tape. The tears came again. Jeff leaned over and gave me a warm hug. "It's going to be okay," he whispered. I nodded automatically, still unable to speak without snuffling, and then I realized something.

After fifteen years and the death of my mother, I was finally mourning the loss of my father.

NINE

"WHY IS IT that writers never throw anything away?" I asked, taking the next cardboard box from Jeff. We had hurried to the closet as soon as we got Bear off to school and Pookie down for her mid-morning nap. And now, surrounded by the boxes and a cloud of dust, I was just beginning to realize what a big job this was going to be.

"It's one of two things," Jeffry answered. "First, to a writer everything has sentimental value, and second, all writers are packrats. Besides, it's easier to pile stuff on the table than to throw it away."

"Ah, an insight into my housekeeping abilities?"

Jeff looked at our hallway, now filled with the dusty old boxes of junk. He shook his head. "I wouldn't dare. You've seen my office."

There were sixteen large boxes in total. They had all been marked "LES," in big block letters, now fading. Some boxes were ripped; others had water stains from Hurricane Andrew. Mom had insisted that none be repacked, just moved as they were to the new house. They were not all filled with my father's stuff, however. I had no idea what was in most of them, and sorting through them was sure to be a long and dirty job. Still, I remained optimistic that we would get through the boxes within a day.

But five hours later we had done only three boxes. It seemed they had all been packed randomly: the box I had just finished, for example, had photographs of Dad with Hubert Humphrey on the top, followed by my sister's third-grade report card—all A's, of course. Next came love letters between my grandfather Clarence Hemingway and grandmother Grace Hall, mixed in with copies of Dad's newspaper, the *Bimini Out-Island News.*

But at the bottom, after sorting through an amazing amount of strange flotsam and jetsam, some of it dating back to the last century—we made the big discovery at last. I think I whispered, "My God." Whatever I said, it was just loud and intense enough to get Jeff's attention.

"What is it?" he said, looking up from a box filled with old stamps and family letters.

I handed him a number of yellowed onionskin pages. "Do you recognize these?"

He looked them over, then caught the title. "Jesus Christ," he said, and read it aloud. " 'The Cannibal Dogs of El Kamir.' "

"Yep." I handed him a second set of pages clipped together. "And this one must be that great snake story, 'Death Stared at Me from Eye Level.' "

"You're kidding," Jeff laughed. "You mean he's telling the professor stories that he wrote?"

"Yeah," I said, and I was filled with conflicting emotions, one of them disappointment, and I guess that's the one that showed in my voice. "I guess that explains it—why he had all the details and all. It was fiction, stuff he'd already researched and written."

"It explains nothing," Jeffry said. "Your father wrote what he lived. So far, both of us have been listening to the tape and not really believing he did these things. But now," he waved the sheaf of papers at me, "now I'm not so sure."

"Well, I am."

"Are you?" Jeff asked. "Everything he wrote in the Bimini newspaper was real. His biography was real, even his novel *Sound of the Trumpet* was true. In fact, I remember your mom telling me that Ernest's criticism of the book was that it was pure reporting. Your dad didn't even change the names. What if these wild hunts really did take place in the thirties and forties? He wrote them up, then retold them to this professor?"

"That's a pretty big what-if." I thumbed through the collection and found the tiger and crocodile stories.

"Well, we have another hour before Bear gets home from school. She made me promise we'd wait for her before we listened to any more of the tape."

"It's all new to her," I said. "I should have told her more— it's her family, too. It's the whole suicide thing. I didn't want to get into that mess with her."

"You still haven't gotten over it," Jeff said.

I took a deep breath and looked at all the boxes stacked around us, all I had left of my father. Jeffry leaned over and wiped a dust smudge from my face. "Maybe that's why your mom gave you this tape. She was the smartest woman I ever knew. Maybe she thought the tape might help. And maybe now it's time to sort things out."

"SO ARE YOU GOING to tell us if Papa ever bedded this woman?" the professor asked as the tape began again.

"What's he mean, bedded?" Bear asked, settling in on the couch in the living room.

"Shhh," I said, and glanced at Jeff, who was all grins. "Keep the questions until the end. Then I'll go over everything."

"You sound like my teacher," Bear said. I leaned over and gave her a hug and we all listened as my father's voice picked up the story again.

"Let me explain what happened after we got to Mogadishu," Dad began.

"There was only one decent little hotel in this East African town. The first thing we did after talking to the town's constable about the attack was to head for the hotel bar. Ernest bought the first round of drinks and the good doctor bought the next."

"What was everyone drinking?" the professor asked.

"Well, they didn't have any decent gin, but the bartender showed Papa his finest brandy. A French cognac called Castillon. Not bad, but as with most things, Papa knew the right way and he wanted to teach everybody how to drink it properly."

"How hard is it to drink brandy?" the professor protested.

"Anybody can slug it, but Papa had learned in Cuba how to do it in a style called *carburación,* based on the same principle of how good engines run better with good mixtures. So picture us sitting at the hotel bar. Not a big place, just room for six people. The wife and doctor were doing their best to unwind. So Papa starts coaching, "To do *carburación* right, you have to take a large mouthful of brandy. Good, Miss Lori, now don't swallow it. Instead swish it around for half a minute or so.

Then, exhaling through the nose, blow all the air out of your lungs. Good. Now, Doctor, swallow the cognac, inhale deeply, and open your mouth quickly. Everyone."

"Bravo," the doctor said, looking up with a wonderful smile. "It enters the lungs in a fine mist and thus goes into the bloodstream faster. Marvelous."

"That's the idea," Papa told him.

Over the next hour two of these fine bottles disappeared as our group sat there making breath-sucking sounds like a school of dying porpoises. Of course there was some small talk; not about the dead hunter and guide, or the dogs. Oddly, the doctor felt a need to talk about literature. It so surprised Papa that he even answered the man.

They had been talking about short stories, which Brown thought was a declining art. "How do you feel about Anderson, Callahan, and Faulkner?" he asked.

"I don't compete with those punks," Papa told him. "Faulkner always goes for the damned fine first paragraph. He gets it often enough, too. But that's it, he fakes the rest. Morley was damned honest, but dull. Hell, he's still dull."

"What about Sherwood Anderson?" Brown wanted to know.

Papa looked at him hard, trying to see if the Doctor knew that this was a loaded question. Then he shrugged and answered. "Since they say I learned everything from Sherwood, I won't criticize him," he said. "But the funny thing, Sherwood and I both learned it from the same place. And that's not Miss Stein, but where Stein got it."

"Where's that?" the doctor asked.

"Huckleberry Finn," Papa answered, laughing. "Damn, Twain was great. He wrote some fine stories."

They went on talking about Twain, and even Hawthorne, for some time before the doctor finished his last drink and announced he was dead tired. It was close to one A.M. when he headed off to his room. I thought it surprising that his wife didn't go with him—and perhaps more surprising that Papa sent me off to bring in our gear from the jeep. This left him and the wife alone in the bar.

I have no idea what they talked about. And if her own husband saw fit to leave her down there in the bar in a strange and wild city, I wasn't the man to worry about it.

Outside, I found that the morning dew had started to settle on our gear. I packed up and took an inventory of what we had left. A couple of high-powered rifles, anti-snakebite serum, chemicals for purifying drinking water, clothes for warm and cold, depending on altitude. Rain jackets, though the heavy rains had already stopped. Several cartons of solid-jacket and soft-nose bullets of different weights and velocities. We could still hunt anything from elephants, rhinos, and buffaloes to the thinner-skinned game like tigers and warthogs.

"Wait a minute, did Ernest bed the wife?" interrupted the professor.

"Cut to the chase," my mother murmured in the background.

"That's the funny part," Dad said. "She wanted him to, very badly. She stayed on at the bar hanging on Papa's every word for the whole half-hour while I pulled the gear up to our room. But when I came back it was clear that Papa was finished with this woman."

"Did he explain why?"

"It's impossible to understand the workings of another man's mind. Even your own brother's. Maybe the woman's behavior toward her husband had soured Papa's infatuation, beauty being only skin-deep. And people forget that he had a strong streak of old-fashioned morality, too, and I won't say that had no effect. But most of all, I think Papa found her curious. He was studying her to try to understand the kind of woman that holds on to a man simply for status and money. It was clear she lacked respect and love. She was a special kind of witch."

"How did it end?"

"He sent her back to her husband. She must have been disappointed; we heard later that she told the doctor she had been naughty anyway. She was capable of saying anything to drive the poor bastard crazy. But when it was over, Papa liked the doctor."

"Maybe that's why he wrote 'The Short Happy Life of Francis Macomber' the way he did. It would have been kinder if she had shot him."

"Perhaps. We didn't stick around to find out. Papa suggested we leave the hotel bar and get some fresh air. We walked only about four blocks and found a warehouse full of people. Papa thought it was a local boxing match, but after we entered we realized it was a very different sporting event."

"Ah, the rats," I heard my mother say.

"The what?" asked the professor.

"Rats," said Charlie Willeford without missing a beat. "The famous rat fights of Mogadishu. Surely you've heard of them?"

"Ah, no, not actually," the professor admitted.

"Hard to believe," my mother said.

"Tell him, Les," Charlie went on. "Tell him about the fighting rats of Mogadishu."

"Yes, please do," said the professor, and he sounded a little dubious. "I've never heard of anything like it."

"It wasn't so much the rats," my dad began after a suitable pause.

The room was clouded with cigar smoke. The crowd of maybe two hundred sat along low bleachers facing three men in the center of the room. The three were bent over a wooden enclosure about the size of a baby's playpen. The four low walls and open roof gave it an innocent appearance, but anyone who looked around the room would realize that the pen had been placed there for a different purpose.

Surrounding the pen, the bleachers were jammed close together, spectators leaning forward, following the actions of the men standing opposite them. The crowd was a wild mixture, the way only a crowd in North Africa can be—everything from Arabs to Zulus crammed into the bleachers. A babble of excited voices in two dozen languages filled the room, and the air of expectancy made it apparent that something unusual was about to happen.

From a long heavy cage balanced upon a wall of the pen and supported by one man came rustling noises and high, reedy squeals. Inside, you could see small dark bodies pressing against the wire, tumbling about, searching frantically for escape. A noise from the cage brought an answering sound, a dog's low growl, full of anger and impatience. It echoed and then died away, and the room was suddenly quiet. The crowd edged closer in anticipation.

A sliding door of the cage was pulled back, and in the instant writhing bodies plummeted into the pen.

"Christ, Baron, is that what I think it is?" Papa asked. He didn't have on his glasses, and his eyesight was poor in the dark.

"Looks like rats," I answered.

As the first body dropped to the floor a man began counting in the native tongue, in clear, booming tones that carried through the entire room. The numbers sounded, perfectly timed to the thud of each small body. The count mounted steadily, the numbers followed by falling and scraping noises in the pen. The announcer passed ninety and still continued, but when his voice sounded one hundred it stopped with an abrupt finality.

Papa and I edged closer. We could see the cage door close with a snap, and the murmuring broke out again as the crowd of men settled back into their seats. Papa gave two of the locals a wad of bills and we were quickly given front-row seats.

"Like the Cuban cockfights, only with rats," he said with a laugh.

"The rats fight each other?" I asked.

"No," he answered and pointed to a short, bearded man leading a small dog toward the center of the room. It was a terrier, staring anxiously at the pit and straining on its leash as it approached.

"In a few moments," Papa whispered, "we're going to see a battle to the death, kid."

BEAR THUMPED THE STOP BUTTON.

"Wait a minute," she demanded. "Is this for real? They're going to put a little dog in a cage full of rats?"

"I think that's the general idea," I said.

"That's horrible!" Bear said.

"Yes, it is."

"Why didn't your daddy make them stop?"

"Honey, he was a stranger, and in a foreign country. There was a big crowd of pretty rough customers around him who wanted to see the fight. There wasn't much he could do."

"He should have done something," she said stubbornly.

"Maybe he did," Jeff said, and Bear looked up at him with hope. "Let's listen to the rest of the story."

She frowned, then nodded. "Okay," she said, reaching for the Play button, and adding in a whisper, "Come on, Grandpa."

I looked down at the pit teeming with rats.

"The odds are a hundred to one," Papa said. "Not good for the dog." I knew he was right. The thought of a fight this unfair made my stomach turn. "No dog should be treated like this," I said.

"Don't count the dog out, Baron. It may not have nine lives, but terriers are natural ratters." A Berber leaned over to Papa, and with some vigorous sign language and a few words of mutual French, they placed a bet. Obviously, Papa was content to go along with the spirit of the event. Maybe he had traveled so much that this didn't seem so damned foreign to him, but I couldn't stomach the thought of watching that dog fed to the rats and then betting on it.

Still, there was not a hell of a lot I could do. And as Papa had said, it wouldn't do to count out the terrier before the fight. He was straining at his leash and seemed eager to give it a try. So I thought, what the hell. This whole African trip had been a series of life lessons. And despite the fact that rat-baiting was one of the original indoor sports of old cities, I was more used to today's sporting events that pitted man against man. Baseball, football, and boxing. But I knew damned well that there were plenty of people who thought those sports were barbaric.

So I tried to relax, to watch and learn. I looked the crowd over. All around the room large sums of money were quickly changing hands.

"Think of it as nature's theater," Papa whispered when he saw my concern.

"Sure," I answered. I knew the English had bear-baiting. It was the favorite of both noble and commoner for centuries. The bear was placed in a pit with as many as twenty dogs, and usually emerged victorious, mangling or killing his tormentors with his sharp claws and powerful jaws. But this kind of thing was not entertainment for me.

"Wait a minute," the professor asked, "did Papa know about your dislike of this sport?"

"I think he sensed it," Dad answered. "He told me how the fox terrier was the only breed of dog that was unintimidated by the most overwhelming odds. And how terriers were used to hunt rats in the big cities in Europe even a hundred years ago. He said the speed of terriers, with their slashing teeth and jaws like steel traps, gave them an edge."

"Did he change your opinion?"

"Hell, no. I didn't care about the dog's advantages. And I didn't care that this kind of sport supported a community of jobs from the gamblers to dog trainers to rat catchers."

The professor laughed. "And just how does one catch a hundred live rats?"

"You really want to know?"

"By all means," the professor answered.

"In Mogadishu, the rat catchers get the local blacksmiths to make tongs about a yard in length with a fattened end for grasping the rats, and then they hunt them in the stinking sewers. They can bring in as many as three hundred rats in an evening. Papa and I saw one of these catchers on our way out. His rats were in a burlap bag and he kept shaking it to prevent them from gnawing their way out. The fight promoter pays him twelve cents for each grown rat."

"Hell of a way to make a living," my mother said.

"Almost as bad as being an English professor," Willeford chuckled.

"True. Tell me Les, what happened to this little dog?" the professor asked.

"The dog had a strange Swahili name, but Papa renamed

him Littledog. A terrier champion who had from birth been trained for one purpose only—to be a rat-killing machine. He was brutally efficient, merciless, and completely without fear. It's no wonder that Papa adopted him."

"He what?"

"Adopted him, or bought him, and for good reason. I'll tell you why in a moment, but first I'm going to tell you this little dog's story. The dog's owner wouldn't sell the dog until after he had told it to Papa. Which was fair, since Papa wanted to know the kind of training that goes into an animal like this."

TEN

WHEN THIS DOG was five weeks old, he was bigger and stronger than any other in his litter. In the rough-and-tumble play of puppy life, Littledog had shown himself to be the quicker and more aggressive, winning all the mock fights within his litter.

Then his owner and trainer took him to a new home, a pit. And Littledog began the daily routine of exercise. His meals of raw meat were given at the same time every day, and at the same time three full-grown rats whose teeth had been removed were also placed in the pit. This was so Littledog would grow up roughing them up without the fear of retaliation. And also so he could get used to the reward of fresh meat when he saw the rats.

The day arrived when Littledog received a painful surprise, one that tested his mettle. He had become accustomed to treating his rat playmates with contemptuous roughness, nipping them with his teeth, tumbling them about, and holding them in his strong jaws while he slapped them against the sides of the pit. They had always submitted to his punishment without the least resistance.

But one day a new rat was dropped to the floor, and Littledog began his usual tactics. In a flash the rat turned on him, hissing angrily, and its sharp teeth sank into his side. Littledog retreated to the end of the pit, dismayed by this unforeseen resistance. The rat still had its upper teeth; only the lowers had been removed.

The trainer watched anxiously from the sidelines. Here was the first chance to find out whether Littledog had what it takes. If he refused to fight, all the training was wasted, and his owner would have to look elsewhere for his rat-pit champion.

But Littledog's retreat didn't last very long. He gave a low growl, and in one leap grabbed the rat by the throat. There was a quick shake of his head, a snap of his jaws, and the rat's neck was broken. He hurled it against the side of the pit and then looked to his trainer for praise.

His trainer told him in his native tongue, "Good boy. We're going to make money together."

When Littledog was six months old he was tried out on full-grown rats with their teeth intact. As in professional fights, he was dropped into the pit with the rats. He showed no fear, and when he was able to dispose of five without trouble, the number was increased to ten. When that was no problem, his owner decided he was ready for his first regulation fight.

In this contest before spectators, Littledog killed ten rats in only five minutes, and from then on he was pitted against larger and larger numbers until he learned to face one hundred rats without a tremor.

The night we had come to this contest, there were two bouts scheduled with an intermission. We had missed the first bout and arrived at the end of the intermission.

Around Papa and me, the spectators and owners were making heavy wagers on which of the two dogs would dispose of one hundred rats in the fastest time. Papa found out that if a man gambled right, he could earn a year's salary on that one bet.

Littledog was at the height of his career. But he had been matched against a dog whose feats equaled his own.

We stared at the portable rat-pit in the center of the room. It was wood on the outside and it had a smooth tin lining on the inside to keep the rats from climbing out to escape.

The first dog's time had been fourteen minutes. Now it was Littledog's chance to better that. His owner held him above the pit and stroked and petted him. He whispered praise to him in Swahili.

"Look at Littledog," Papa said. "He can see the rats being dropped into the pit and he wants them."

"He's a fool. It takes one bite to the eye and the dog is blind, or one to the neck and the dog will bleed to death."

"If you want to root for the underdog, Baron, root for the rats. Littledog will win. I can see it."

And I believe he could see it. Papa had the absolute ability to look at two competitors and pick the winner every time. Me—all I saw were frenzied rats that fought wildly with each other, bunching together in twirling heaps. It was impossible for the trainer to find an open spot to drop the dog. But after a minute, the close-packed mass separated. Rats began scrambling up the smooth sides of the walls, leaping and falling back to the floor. There was a clear place in the middle, and the small dog was dropped quickly.

The old bell on the table rang and the battle was on. In a flash Littledog seized the first rat by the throat, snapped his jaws, and flung it away. Littledog's owner groaned. The rat, an enormous brown veteran of many rat-pack fights, had not been killed, and with a squeal of rage it joined the crowd now surging over Littledog. He was lost from our sight in the torrent of dark rat bodies that covered him.

"That's it," I said to Papa. "Littledog is through. Ironic, isn't it? Seven hours ago we watched wild dogs pull a man apart, and now we're watching rats pull a dog apart."

"Life's cheap in Africa. Never forget that, Baron. Never."

After all I had been through, how could I forget it? I had learned well just how cheap my own life was. But just then Papa's Littledog started to show his training and fighting heart. His head emerged from the mad melee of wild rats, and his steel jaws could be seen snapping in all directions, every opening and closing motion bringing death to a foe.

"There's my boy," Papa said excitedly. "Look, there's no wasted effort; each time he snaps his teeth together, his neck swivels and another dead rat is hurled against the wall."

"Yes," I answered, "but I can also see the blood streaming from quite a few cuts on Littledog's body. He's sure to have rabies by now. Even if he lives."

We watched as Littledog went on with his savage killing. Every ounce of his energy was used in his life-and-death battle.

By now the floor of the pit was a pool of blood. As the heaps of broken bodies piled higher, the remaining rats, panic-stricken, refused to fight. They careened about the pit in senseless flight, scrambling desperately up the tin walls only to fall back into the dog's waiting jaws.

The dog's owner bent over the timekeeper's watch. Ten minutes had passed and he signaled the crowd the time and that there were now only three rats left alive in the pit.

But I could see that one of those three was the wily veteran who had eluded Littledog before, and was dodging too cleverly to be caught. The remaining two made the mistake of huddling in a corner and in a sudden leap the little dog slashed one across the throat, snapped its neck, and flung it aside, dead. He then seized the other, which hissed in terror. A quick crunch of the dog's jaws and it was dying, its dark body twisting and quivering against the wall.

The dog's owner glanced at the timekeeper's watch again. Eleven minutes for ninety-nine rats! Papa's Littledog had a chance to establish an all-time record. Would he do it?

Only one rat was left, but now there was plenty of room for maneuvering, and a deadly game of sudden shifts, furious lunges, and wild leaps began. Littledog stalked his prey from wall to wall, trying every trick he knew. Once, after a feint in one direction, he spun at the rat's throat from the other side. The brown veteran escaped death by the narrowest margin. The dog's owner clapped a hand to his head as the dog, slipping on the bloody floor, missed his grip and the rat scrambled away.

Papa checked his own watch: another half-minute had elapsed. "It's now eleven and a half minutes. My boy can still win if he can get that last clever rat."

The duel continued, dog and rat sliding and clambering over the bodies strewn around the pit. Then the rat made his fatal mistake. Cornered in a surprise shift, he chose to leap high against the side of the pit, hoping to come down near another wall. There was a sharp crack as his head hit the metal rim. He landed on the floor, momentarily stunned.

"Go, boy!" Papa yelled. And lightning fast, Littledog was on the rat. There was one futile effort at escape and then the terrier's jaws closed. A twist of the head, a savage fling, and the bout was over.

"Twelve minutes! Twelve minutes!" The timekeeper shouted, as the bell rang again and again. The crowd was on its feet whistling and stamping. Papa's Littledog had set what proved to be an unbeatable record in rat-pit fighting. No other dog—terrier or other breed—to my knowledge ever equaled his time of twelve minutes for the slaughter of one hundred rats.

I remember Papa saying, "I want that dog. I want him to catch rats and to sire handsome puppies."

"Was the dog to replace his cats in Key West?" the professor interrupted.

"What cats? Papa never had cats in Key West. Don't tell me you bought into that six-toed feline nonsense? Look closely at the pictures of Papa with cats. You'll see he's older and living in Cuba. Pauline kept peacocks in Key West. And Papa didn't have cats in Key West out of respect for those birds."

"But there are so many stories about Hemingway's six-toed cats," the professor protested.

"Who doesn't love a good story? Especially tourists."

"What about the famous urinal?"

"The urinal might have come from Sloppy's, or when they remodeled the old fort. But it wasn't for the cats. Pauline fixed it up for her birds. Those lovely, loud-as-hell peacocks. Now I'm *not* saying Papa didn't like cats. He did. He used to say, 'A cat has absolute emotional honesty.' People hide their feelings for various reasons, but cats never do."

"No cats? But—you're sure?"

"For Christ's sake, I was there. Of course I'm sure. Absolutely sure. They're just not real. No cats."

"Why didn't we hear about this dog in Key West? I know about the dog in Cuba, a black springer spaniel. I think he called it Black Dog?"

"Correct. Black Dog was a great dog. Loyal to the end. In fact he showed his loyalty by confronting some of Castro's guerrillas who came to Papa's house looking for guns. He was a blind old dog and never saw what hit him. But Papa found part of a cracked rifle butt near Black Dog's body and lodged an official complaint with the Batista government. A lot of good that did."

"Not to change the subject, but what happened to Papa's champion, Littledog?"

"Well, as I told you, Papa bought the dog, for close to two hundred dollars. He had every intention of taking it back to Key West. He said, 'This is the kind of dog all writers need. A ratter, perfect for turning loose on any gathering of critics.' "

"But the dog never made it to Key West?" the professor asked.

"No. After the fight, we took Littledog back to the hotel. Gave him a bath and Papa looked over his wounds. The rat bites had caused Littledog's head and body to swell. After a couple more days the swelling went down, but Customs said we would have to put Littledog in quarantine for a year. Papa couldn't bring himself to do that to this fine animal. He left Littledog with a friend who promised he would be well cared for. The friend later wrote saying Littledog had fully recovered from his injuries."

MY DAUGHTER STOPPED the tape and said, "I want to know about the cats. I mean, we always play with them in Key West. Why aren't they real?"

"They're real cats," Jeff said, laughing. "They're just not descended from any pet of your great-uncle's."

I could see the confusion on Bear's face. Since she'd been born, we had always gone to Key West in the summer. As a child, I too had chased the Hemingway cats. I had grown up knowing and liking Bernice Dixon, the owner of the Hemingway House and Museum. But when I got older, I also had heard the cats were not Ernest's.

"The cats aren't so bad," Jeff said. "Tell Bear about the barstool scam."

"The what?" Bear asked.

I shook my head. "There were at least a dozen folks over the years who claimed to have bought Ernest Hemingway's bar stool."

"The only bar stool that Hemingway ever sat on in Key West," Jeff said. "In how many years? And he only sat on one stool?"

"Then why did they say he did?" Bear asked.

"Someone down there was just running a racket—selling ordinary stools to gullible tourists."

"Just goes to show," Jeff added, "people would rather believe the made-up stories than the real ones. Though after listening to this tape—I'm not sure I know what's real and what's not anymore."

"Let's keep going," I said, and started the tape player again.

ELEVEN

"Tell me—" the professor began. There was a pause and a clink of ice on glass. I guessed he was taking a sip of his drink. Was he starting to feel more comfortable? Would he turn into an actual human being? "Of all the strange animals you and Papa hunted, which one stands out in your mind as the greatest hunt?"

"Do you mean most unusual?" Willeford asked.

"Or the scariest?" my father rumbled.

"I think what I'm looking for is the one that perhaps taught you the most about hunting or about your relationship with your brother," the professor answered.

"That's an awfully tall order," my mom said with a laugh. "But hands-down it has to be the one that left you with the scar."

"Scar? What kind of scar?" the professor asked, and after a pause added, "What are you doing?"

"I'm rolling up my pants leg." There was a sound of movement. I pictured my father's legs, pale in the light of his ceremonial fire. "Look," he said. "See this? I lost my entire damn ankle on this hunt."

"My God."

"No, not God. Just damn bad luck. Look—see how the scar tissue is uneven, feel that."

"Yuck."

"Yeah, that's where the gangrene set in. You know what causes this kind of wound?"

"No," the professor answered.

"Well, it's the most unusual animal to hunt, and plenty scary, too—ask yourself if you could trust your brother to hack off the meat on your ankle if it meant saving your life."

"Ernest did this?" the professor asked.

"He didn't have a choice, it was the Far East," Willeford answered.

"Exactly. In 1941, Papa was sent to write about British defenses there. I got to tag along and write a story for a men's adventure magazine."

"The great Komodo Dragon hunt," my mom said matter-of-factly.

"Good lord, Ernest Hemingway went dragon hunting?" the professor asked. "That hardly seems to be in his league."

"What? You don't think dragons are serious business?" my father demanded.

"Well, it doesn't really seem on a par with the tigers," the professor said.

"Komodo Dragons aren't just large lizards. They are serious predators. But before we get too far, I want to say, we started this trip with no intention of hunting anything. And so we were ill-prepared, and that's where the real danger lay."

It was the spring of 1941 when Papa, myself, and Martha, my third favorite sister-in-law and a first-rate war correspondent in her own right, flew east. First to San Francisco, then to Honolulu, Midway, Wake, Guam, Manila, Hong Kong, and Singapore. From there, we grabbed the first transport out, but we were misdirected and ended up on a ship that was headed for Flores Island. It was three horrible days of pitching and rolling before we finally made it to the island. We anchored that first night in the island's lee and saw a queer light that filled the evening sky. Its rosy yellows separated the sky from the sea.

I remember Papa asking about that sunset. We were surprised to learn it came from the dust blown all the way over from the great Australian desert. Before the sun went down, we asked the captain about the neighboring islands. He told us the far one was the island of Timor, the closer one was Komodo.

"Komodo? Where the dragon lizards live?" I asked. I had been researching reptiles just a few weeks earlier for a magazine pitch, but I never thought I would get the chance to come face to face with a real dragon lizard.

"The very same," the captain answered.

Papa's eyes lit up. "What a fine hunt that would make, Baron. Think of it, we'd be dragon-slayers."

"That would go over big with the fair maidens," I said.

So at dinner, Papa brought the idea up to Martha, or Marty as he called her. Much to my surprise, Lady Marty also liked this idea. As for me, I had always had a fascination with this whole area. After all, these were the islands where Captain Bligh of *Mutiny on the Bounty* fame arrived. Add to that the experience of a lifetime, hunting real dragons. It was a grand idea, and I couldn't wait to get started.

After dinner we walked along the ship's deck to discuss what we would need for this venture. I remember the sky and ocean had become an inky black. A voice from the darkness behind us spoke. "Those are rough territories. You'll need some real firepower for a large lizard." My eyes fixed on the glow of a cigarette in the darkness.

"What do you have in mind?" Papa asked the burning cigarette.

"I have two heavy rifles. They're .505 Mannlichers with plenty of cartridges." The dull glow of the cigarette grew brighter. "I'll make you a good deal."

"I'm listening," Papa answered.

"Two hundred rupian each."

"Done," Papa agreed, "but only if you also arrange safe passage to the island for us."

Just then we heard muffled drumming coming over the water. We all turned to the black sea. Finally Lady Marty asked, "What is that noise?"

"That—" answered our skipper, stepping from the darkness into the cabin's light, "is your ride. A native *prau,* and if I'm not mistaken she'll shoot right up beside us and set anchor for the night."

"Why the thrumming? Is it some kind of oriental engine?" Papa asked.

"The oldest engines in history," the skipper answered. "It's a drum, or probably two drums. You can make them both out if you listen. She is drumming for wind."

"Does she need more wind than the heavy breeze today?" Martha asked. "I thought we were going to roll over from that little sail you rigged forward."

"Those drums are old—very old. No one knows how long they've been doing this, but they always drum when they want a wind. Even when they have it. It's a kind of insurance—for tomorrow."

In the next few moments the thrumming grew louder. We moved to the starboard side and faced the rhythmic beat that pulsated through the darkness. But no matter how hard we stared at the black ocean, we saw nothing.

Then finally—"I see something," Martha said, pointing off our bow. "So do I," Papa agreed. And I too could vaguely see a darker blackness on the surface of the sea. It seemed to be coming closer. Then it was a definite something as it crossed the path of two low-rising stars. It wavered and I knew then that those were the sails, gently flapping as the *prau* came into the wind. There was a splash and their anchor set down.

"Ahoy there," I shouted down. A lantern appeared aft. It was the first light we'd seen on the little boat.

"Ahoy, Tuans," the call came back.

Our skipper patted my shoulder. "He's a good man, he can get you to the lizards in the morning. You'll see." The skipper then went forward to lower a boat down.

Within fifteen minutes we'd all piled in and rowed over to the *prau*. The old man who was the *prau*'s captain told our skipper he would carry us over to Dragon Island, but that we would have to wait for the breeze to come up.

"How does he know we'll get any wind? It may be calm," Martha asked the skipper, who was working as our interpreter.

"Don't worry, pretty woman," the *prau* captain said in translation. "It will be a fine day. Did you not hear us drumming up the breeze for tomorrow?"

And that settled that, at least for the moment.

At first light we were on the *prau* headed for Komodo Island. I could hardly believe it. The mountains that had seemed such soft, purple shapes the night before were now sharp brown peaks, far inland. And between the peaks were miles of green and yellow vegetation. We were headed for the sandy beach with its line of thin, tall palm trees.

Before we could touch the sand we had to get through the barrier of reefs that stretched the last mile ahead of us. Then suddenly, we were swept over one breaking spot. I could see the great coral reef below, its jagged edges reaching out to our ship. We passed over it with few bumps and then we were in calm water, the windward reef safely behind us. I turned to Papa. "Deadly water, but lovely," I said.

"None lovelier," he agreed.

We could see native huts on the beach, and a dozen figures running along the shallows and hauling in a large fishing net. The *prau*'s captain swung the tiller down, and the boat shot up into the wind and lay fluttering like a wounded bird in the brilliant sunshine. She was well within the outer reef, and had plenty of mottled green water around her.

"Now for those large lizards," Papa said, picking up our newly acquired rifles.

"Don't you mean dragons?" Martha laughed.

But Papa had already turned away to talk to the captain. He wanted to make sure the *prau* would be there to pick us up the following day. This he did by ripping a hundred-rupian note in half. Half he gave to the old captain with a certain amount of sign language; the other half he placed in his shirt pocket. The captain nodded and showed his three teeth in a smile. He understood that on our return he would get the other half of the bill. I grabbed our bags and we disembarked to a dugout canoe that took us ashore.

Papa walked with the local who had rowed us in. He used more sign language, then nodded and passed the man a few Indonesian banknotes. Turning to Lady Marty, he said, "We have a hut for the night."

Martha and I looked ahead to the huts along the beach. They were a scrawny lot. "Well, at least it has a roof," I told her.

"Yes, but I'm guessing no room service," Martha said, laughing.

Papa rejoined us. "Okay, Baron, we've got the evening and the early morning to bag a dragon. Let's not waste it."

After a brief stop in the village, where we found a couple of horses and one of the locals to serve as a guide, we rode up into the hills. The guide showed us the wild-pig tracks running everywhere. From what I had read in the zoological study back home, I knew Komodo dragons love pig meat. I also knew the cannibals in the South Pacific often called human flesh "long pig," because of the similar tastes. "If we can get a couple of hogs, we could set them out as dragon bait," I suggested.

"Great idea, Baron," Papa said. "I'll give you first shot for the swine."

Of course I agreed, and that one decision changed my life.

TWELVE

WE RODE a little farther, until we came to a deep ravine. There were scurrying noises coming from the heavy brush about fifty yards ahead. I got off my horse and waited the animal out. A sixty-pound wild boar drew its head from a shaded overhang. I paused for a moment, then squeezed the trigger. The hills echoed with a loud *ca-ra-wong*.

I'd hit the boar on the right side of his head. It was a clean shot that buckled his legs and propelled him back with a two-ton shock, dead before he hit the ground.

"Nice shooting," Papa said, grinning.

"A bit of overkill, but a clean kill," I agreed. "I'll get him," I said, handing my gun to Lady Marty. That was a big mistake. Because now I was unarmed as I ran toward the pig. I had just assumed that if anything attacked, Papa would shoot it. I would have done the same for him. But I was about to discover Hemingway Life Lesson Number 101, a new rule for me: Never believe in anyone more than in yourself.

I never saw that great lizard in the brush, not even as I ran past it. But after I went by, the beast gave chase. It's a reflex with most predators. They'll chase anything that runs from them. I heard rocks scraping under some heavy foot, and thinking Papa was following me for some reason, I looked back and saw a huge blur of green-brown closing in. I felt like a rabbit discovered by a big dog. This was his yard and I had foolishly entered it.

I didn't even have time to turn and face the thing before he was on me. The dragon grabbed my right foot and sent me sprawling to the ground. I tried to pull away, but the animal shook its head to let me know he had a solid grip. The pain was incredible, but the stink of that thing's breath was worse. And even worse was how helpless I felt. I was sure Papa would kill the thing, save my bacon, but the seconds dragged on and the dragon kept its grip on my leg, and the cavalry didn't show up.

Why didn't Papa shoot? What was he waiting for? A thousand questions go through your mind at a time like this, until suddenly, with absolute clarity, you have the answer—help yourself, or die.

With my good foot I stomped the beast as hard as I could in the snout. On the third kick, the dragon let go and stepped back, shaking its head, left and right. Its tongue flicked in and out as if to taste my fear. Was it going to attack again? My ankle was a mess, and I knew I couldn't run.

Why hadn't Papa shot?

For one of the longest moments of my life the great reptile stared at me. There was nothing in those cold eyes, not the faintest gleam of anything in common like you might see in the eyes of any mammal predator. Just cold, lizard eyes with no feeling. I stared back, bracing for the shock of that huge body slamming me to the ground.

And then for reasons I still don't know, the huge dragon turned away, and moved off into the bushes.

Moments later Papa reached me. "Are you all right, Baron?" he asked as he helped strip off my ragged boot.

"I'm not sure. The damn thing chewed my foot." I pointed back toward the tall grass. "He went in there."

Papa paused and listened. We heard Martha and the local guide coming closer with the horses and then—a soft, hardly perceptible sound—breathing.

"He's still there. He's watching us," whispered Papa. He lifted the Mannlicher toward a pair of yellow eyes hiding in the green. A lizard tongue shot out of the brush.

"Dragon bastard," I said fighting the pain now pulsing in my foot. My eyes made out the beast's from his camouflaged surrounding, just as Papa cracked back the bolt and worked a cartridge into the chamber. The sound of the oiled mechanism didn't seem to bother the animal. Papa aimed high on the shoulder and—*ca-ra-wong!*

The shot echoed off the hillside and the horses reared back, but my eyes were glued to the wild thrashing in the grass. I remember the snout of the beast smacking a small tree and knocking it over. From my perspective on the ground I had no idea how big the dragon truly was, but from the way the grass and brush moved it had to be nine feet from nose to tail.

Martha ran up to Papa, who had chambered in a second round. She held my gun and they both stood between me and the dragon. Little comfort when I realized I couldn't move even if I wanted to. The animal's huge tail swung out from the brush. His short muscular legs dug their claws into a dead tree and the lizard lifted itself over in a last-ditch effort to leave. Papa's shot had not killed him. It had only convinced him it was time to give up dinner. "He's getting away," Martha said.

"The hell he is," Papa countered and fired again.

This time, my brother hit his mark. The dragon's head swung up, and blood spilled from a wound there. The beast fell over dead in the brush.

Martha broke the silence. "Old Hem, you dragon-slayer."

"Damn right." Papa grinned and moved in toward his kill. The local man helped pull the animal out into the clearing. Its feet were as big around as baseball mitts, each with five deadly two-inch claws.

"He'll make a fine trophy, Baron," Papa said, finally turning back to me. It was then that he noticed my condition. "Oh, damn—how the hell is the foot?"

"Not so good," I answered.

Papa and Martha came over. Beads of sweat were rolling down my cheeks. I held my gray sock up. It was soaked red. My ankle had three deep tooth marks scraped across it. "I can't feel my toes and there's considerable pain in the leg."

Papa pulled his belt off. "Quit complaining. It looks bad, but it's just a lousy lizard bite."

"A sizable lizard," I protested. "A dragon."

"Are dragons poisonous?" Martha asked.

"Not like snakes," I answered. "From what I read, their saliva carries an enzyme that breaks down protein." I took a breath, and fought the rising pain. "It's primitive, but effective. Christ, is it effective."

"Okay, we'll bleed it and disinfect it. You'll be back on your feet by dinnertime."

I didn't know if it was pain, fear, heat, or the effect of that goddamned lizard's bite, but my little voice of reason was screaming, *It's not going to be that easy.*

Papa wound his belt around my leg just below the knee. When it was sufficiently tight, he gave three short twists. I gritted my teeth and let out a few choice American phrases. Papa then opened his pocketknife and cut an X over the wounds so they would bleed clean.

"Lousy lizard spit," he said, "I can't cut more deeply. It's all tendons and bone in there. Tomorrow you'll see the ship's doctor."

"Sorry, Papa," I said, feeling I had messed up everything. "At least you bagged one dragon."

"Damn, the bait. I almost forgot. Maybe we can still set a trap. You'll get your shot, kid."

Before I could tell him no thanks, Papa left for the wild boar. His luck was better than mine and he missed being attacked by any large lizards. By the time he got back, three local men had joined our group.

Our guide motioned them over to look at my wound. The taller man said in his very best English, "Bad—very bad."

My stomach sank. "Not much on bedside manner," Martha kidded. A moment later, the guide and another local hoisted me over their shoulders and put me on a horse headed back toward the settlement. I heard Papa and Martha tell the others to skin out our dragon and set up the bait.

The men put me down inside the hut Papa had rented. Our gear was in a corner on the sand floor. I curled up into a fetal position, my body shaking uncontrollably. "Look, fellas," I said, "I really need some water." I felt another spasm coming on. As I lay shivering, I saw that my leg had puffed up more and had turned grayish-white. This was not a good sign.

A few minutes passed before I realized that I had been left alone in the room. Then all at once everyone seemed to pile in. Papa and Martha, our local guide, and another man who turned out to be the island's medicine man. As Papa searched through our gear, Martha answered my prayers and gave me water.

"We're a little low on disinfectant, Baron," Papa told me as he turned around. "We do have a bottle of Gordon's gin, iodine, and some Band-Aids. So it's going to smart a little." Papa mixed the iodine and Gordon's together.

"A waste of good gin," I answered through gritted teeth. Then he poured the mix across the wounds and I let out a serious yell. The cool of the alcohol did little to calm the heat now coming off the wound. Martha bandaged the wound when she finally got me to hold still.

Papa gave me a toast: "To my little brother, who kicked a dragon into submission. Cheers." Everyone took a drink and after that first shot, I did feel better. Martha gave me a blanket and for the moment the shaking stopped.

"Excuse me, but did Ernest ever offer a reason why he didn't shoot the attacking dragon?" the professor inquired.

"I wanted to ask him—but the moment for questions had passed. What was done was done."

"Oh, but really. Even if you were temporarily deranged from pain, you wanted to know. Why not ask?"

"You have to understand, I know he felt bad. But he would not have admitted it. Remember Papa's saying: 'If you're any damn good, everything is your own damn fault.' Well, balls—I should have taken my gun. I should have been more careful. Life Lesson 101: Never believe in anyone more than in yourself. From that day forward, I never forgot it."

Papa let me rest while he and the others stepped outside our hut to the porch. I remember that the medicine man lingered for a minute looking over my wounds, and then he too left.

Outside, I overheard Papa say, "Do whatever it takes to get that boat back here at first light." He then went on with telling the natives not to waste the kill. And to give us some meat for dinner and the rest for the settlement. We would use only the swine's head and guts for bait.

I know most was understood because I did get a pork dinner. The guide then set out the pig's head, bones, and entrails as bait. He tied two small hand bells to the bucket and placed it some twenty-five yards away from our hut in the tree line.

An hour after we ate, I sat with Papa and Martha. We tried to joke about the accident. I remember Papa looking over at the Mannlicher and saying it was a very unlucky gun. Too heavy to carry well and if I had been shooting with a lighter rifle, like a Springfield, I would have killed the dragon on its charge. True or not, I wanted to believe it.

That evening I drank more than my fair share of the gin, but that was Papa's intention. I finally fell asleep. We had agreed to keep the lantern burning all night, in case we needed to see what was going on, or some other emergency occurred.

Papa and Martha had returned to the porch. She held our only flashlight, while Papa lay the heavy rifle across his lap. I don't know just what time it was when I awoke. I could see their silhouettes on the porch, Martha's head on Papa's shoulder, his arm around her waist. They looked very relaxed, very happy. Hard to believe they would be divorced in just a couple of years.

I think Marty was at her best when she was covering wars. She was so much her own woman. She had already had one book published before ever meeting Papa. When I read it, I was taken by her descriptions, some graphic stuff on man's inhumanity to man. I know Papa and Martha shared the belief that writers should do what they can for human rights and dignity. That was tested when they covered the civil war in Spain. That was where Papa truly fell in love with her.

This trip, however, I could see the beginning of the end. It all came down to competition. True, they worked well together in interviews. On this trip they talked to everyone from British military officers to coolies. They brought into focus their assessments of things to come and were both lucky and astute. They predicted the first attack would come from Japan against American bases in the Pacific.

In the evenings, their hotel room filled with the sounds of two typewriters working. Papa wrote his own material, and worked over Martha's; she in turn copied out his material and they combined their thinking and sometimes their phrases in magazine pieces under one byline or another. It's a rare gift to find another writer that you trust so completely. But that's what these two people had in common. They both wrote damn wonderfully and that's what broke them up. The competition got tougher as Martha's career took off. Papa tried to grab credit for it. Maybe he was right, maybe not. One thing was sure, Martha was not content being just Papa's wife. She was a writer and a war correspondent, before she met him and after.

But now we were far from the war, and the reality of my condition set in. I had a serious infection. The wound dripped with pus. I reached down and felt the heat rising from my skin. The pain was steady and moving up the leg.

From the porch I heard Papa talking in low tones to Marty. "I should have left him in Cuba."

"You know, it's a machismo thing. He's trying to be as brave as you and that's going to get him killed. Be happy he's sleeping now," Martha answered.

"Balls, he's a brave kid. We come from the same stock. Remember my Uncle Tyler? He found that the word Hemingway in Chinese means 'hunter of wolves.' Well, damn it—wolf hunters, dragon hunters, it's all the same. The kid beat the monster off with his one good foot."

"I'm sorry, what I meant was—" Martha began, but then there was the tinkly sound of bells in the distance.

"Shhh—listen," Papa said. Just out beyond the hut, from along the tree line, came the sound again. Hardly audible, but a distinct sound—light bells and crunching bones.

"Grab the light, daughter," Papa whispered.

I could hear Martha fumbling for the flashlight. "Shine it at the bait," Papa said urgently. I moved to better peer out the door and the pain was so strong I had to bite down on my lip. I moaned, but I could see a little.

"Easy, Baron," Papa said, hearing me.

The flashlight's beam cut across the field like an aircraft searchlight. It moved across the rocks as Martha searched for the bait—and found it. I could make out quite clearly a long dark animal. Its head rose up into the beam. Its eyes reflected back like two golden beads. Its tongue flicked out and tasted the air. This second dragon lizard was far bigger than the first.

"Shoot," Martha whispered. Papa chambered a round and raised the rifle to his shoulder. He aimed dead between the eyes and pulled the trigger—*ca-ra-wong!*

The shot echoed and re-echoed across the water and down from the hillside. The animal thrashed in the grass with monstrous turns and then finally fell silent.

No one moved for a moment, and then Martha and Papa ran out to see the size of the great beast. I watched the light bobbing across the field and then moving back and forth across the lizard where it lay. "It's over fifteen feet long," I heard Papa call out. He was as excited as a kid.

Things finally seemed to be going right. One shot, a clean kill. A huge trophy dragon and a very happy Papa. I sank back onto the bed and closed my eyes. My leg was throbbing badly and I could feel the clammy sweat pouring off me, but I was awfully happy for Papa.

When they returned there was a round of drinks and much laughter. After a few minutes, however, I think it was Martha who asked, "What is that foul odor?"

The odor. I smelled it, too. I guess I'd been smelling it for a while, but if Martha hadn't pointed it out I probably wouldn't have realized it. I sure as hell didn't want to smell it. But I did, once Martha brought it to my attention, and I knew what it meant. It was the kind of smell that you will never forget, although you will want to.

"Gangrene," Papa said in a low tone, and suddenly the room seemed very quiet and completely filled with that awful smell. He leaned over my wound and looked at it closely. Then he turned and said something to one of the locals who was standing on the porch. The man nodded and went pelting off into the night. Papa came back and knelt by my bedside. "I'm sorry, kid. But every hour we wait, more meat will die. I've sent for the island medicine man."

I recognized the old man when he entered. The white-haired, olive-skinned loner had been the last one to look at my wounds. Now he carried his medicine bag containing three primitive but effective tools. Honey, mud, and maggots.

Let me tell you, you haven't really lived until a piece of you dies. And you haven't begun to die until you have seen that piece digested.

And so, lying there in that little hut, I began to live and to die for the first time. As I've said, I learned a lot on this trip. For gangrene there's only one thing you truly need to know—it spreads. Gangrene spreads, and if you don't stop the spread it eats you until there is nothing left but a bad smell and a memory. In the nine hours since my attack, the three small puncture marks had grown to an infected area about the size of my fist.

The old man made a face as he looked at my wound. Then he grabbed a handful of something from his bag. Like a priest sprinkling holy water, he shook his hand over the wound. At first I thought the fever was making me see things. But when I looked up and saw Martha's face, I knew it was true. He was dropping hundreds of fat, white, writhing maggots on my leg. I screamed and tried to knock them off. But Papa stopped me. "Easy, Baron. The damned bugs are good for you. They're going to save your leg."

"The hell you say," I protested.

"The hell I do. Maggots only eat dead flesh. They won't touch healthy tissue. Close your eyes! Close your eyes, God damn it!" I struggled one last time and realized he wasn't going to let me go until I finally did as he asked.

"It's God's truth," he whispered close to my ear. "Can you feel the little bastards?"

"Papa, God damn it," I told him, "don't put me through this. If I'm going to lose the leg, then let me die. I won't live without my leg—"

"Baron, for Christ's sake—"

"I mean it, Papa. I won't do it."

"Baron. Tell me what you feel."

I paused. When Papa used that tone, you listened, and you did what he said. So I concentrated on my leg. There was no feeling at all. No movement, no pain, nothing. I admit I was surprised. I expected to be howling in agony, but I felt nothing. I looked up at Papa and shook my head. "I don't feel a thing," I told him.

"Good," Papa said. "What they are eating is absolutely dead." He stood up. "You won't lose the leg, Baron. I promise. I saw this work in Spain. The hardest part is the waiting. That's why I'm telling you to keep your eyes closed. There's nothing that will make your stomach turn inside-out faster than watching the fat little bastards eat."

A few hours later, the medicine man came back and collected the bugs. As he took the last one off I saw that my flesh had been eaten right down to the pulsating, healthy red flesh under the gangrene. There had been no pain from the maggots at all, not even discomfort, except when I had thought about what was going on down there. The wound looked fine. It was cleaner than if a surgeon had worked on it.

But here, my luck ran out. In the center of the wound the dragon had bitten clean through to the ankle bone, and by the off color, we could tell that the poison in the saliva had killed a large chunk of the bone. It had to come out immediately. I wouldn't want to have that operation at Mount Sinai hospital with the best doctors in the country. And now I had to rely on the skill of ordinary humans on a small Pacific island. A tough choice: a witch doctor or my brother.

Papa made his pitch. "Come on, kid. You know me. You know how I helped Dad up at the Ojibway camp."

The Ojibways were Indians who lived less than two miles from our summer cottage. They were the true poor of the area, owning no land and seldom holding jobs for long. They had regular emergencies—stabbings, broken bones, serious infections. Our father, a doctor, had always volunteered his time and medical training to help these people. My brother often went with him. I knew Papa not only admired the Ojibways, he had learned a lot about emergency medicine under primitive conditions from working at their camp with our father.

As for the local medicine man—I will admit he had been

right about the maggots, no matter how wrong it had seemed at the time. But what would he pull out of his medical bag next, and how could I know if it would work, or if it was just superstition? I am not putting down medicine men as a tribe, you understand. I've seen too many things I couldn't explain all over the world, and too many times I've seen it go badly wrong right here in the States when a real U.S. medical doctor should have known better.

But this was my ankle. A part of me. And I didn't want to trust that to a stranger. To lose a leg, never be able to walk properly again—to me, that's a kind of living hell, and I wanted no part of it.

THE TONE OF DADDY'S VOICE was very different here. He wasn't just telling a story. He was reliving an awful moment— and so was I. His words had made my stomach knot up and turn sour.

"A kind of living hell," he had said, to lose a leg.

And to lose two legs? What would that mean to a man ready to die of gangrene rather than lose one leg? It was unthinkable. But Daddy had faced that decision in the last week of his life—faced it and done something about it that, to me, was just as unthinkable. And I had spent the years since trying not to think about that unthinkable decision.

I remembered the craziness Daddy had put us through the week before his death, and it began to make a little more sense.

He had been in the hospital. The doctors told him they didn't think another surgery would work. There was so little blood flow to his legs that even if they put in new veins in the lower half, the flesh of the leg would still die. They told him that they wanted to take off both his legs to save his life.

My mom told me she had been there when they marked his legs for double amputation. She had tried to tell Daddy it would be all right, they would get along fine, but he wasn't having any comfort. Double amputation was not an option. He wouldn't even think about it. Mom said later she was surprised he didn't haul off and punch the weasly little intern who had drawn the marks on his legs for the incisions.

But Daddy just sat there in the hospital bed, Mom had told us, his head tilted to one side like he was listening to an invisible radio. Then he waited calmly for everyone to leave the room. When he was alone, he ripped all the IVs out of his arms and stormed out of the hospital. They wouldn't give him his clothes, so he came home in the hospital gown, his butt hanging out the open back.

He came home and said he was fine now, and he had truly seemed fine, better than he had been in a long while.

He had made it clear. His mind was made up and there was no changing it. He was not going to have a double amputation.

And that left only one choice.

A week later, he took it.

I was beginning to understand.

I blinked back a tear and listened to the tape.

So I made my choice. Papa would cut the bone.

He didn't waste any time once I told him. He just nodded and said, "Keep smiling, kid." He tied both my legs down and sharpened his hunting knife to a fine edge, running it over a flame to sterilize it. He saw me watching and said, "When I was lying in the hospital in Italy, sometimes the pain in my leg would get so bad I wanted to cry. And I found that if I whistled, it wasn't so bad." He held the blade up to look at it, then stuck it back into the flame. "Whistle, Baron. If it gets bad, just whistle. It helps."

"This will help, too," Martha said, and she gave me the last of the gin and a piece of wood to grind my teeth on.

"I'll try to make it quick," he said, but we both knew it would be slow going.

Over the next hour he removed both living and dead bone. I was in and out of consciousness in a clammy red cloud of pain, and twice Martha had to replace the piece of wood between my teeth. When she took out the splintered pieces, I whistled. It did help.

When Papa was done, the island medicine man covered the

wound in honey. By this point I didn't even care. I guess I thought it was funny, because I remember making some joke about how Papa had done such a great job, the leg was now good enough to eat.

Papa clapped my shoulder and told me I was going to be all right. "Honey is a natural antibiotic, Baron," he said. "It'll kill the infection." To tell the truth, I was so far gone at that point I wouldn't have cared if it was chocolate syrup. But it must have worked. I never did get an infection on that wound.

The medicine man put a thin layer of mud on top. That kept the air and germs off. And I fell into a deep sleep, feeling lucky that I had survived both the operation and the emotional turmoil that followed. Because you have to understand, Papa still felt agitated about my foot, and maybe even a little guilty. So in typical big-brother fashion, he gave me a wonderful chewing-out.

"WAIT A MINUTE. HOLD ON," I said, stopping the tape. I was suddenly confused. "I know my father lost part of his ankle, and I know he lost it from gangrene. But it was not from any Komodo dragon."

"What was it?" Bear asked, looking up with a slightly irritated frown, as if I had broken her train of thought.

"Dad was on his boat down in the Caribbean. He was in heavy seas, pulling up the anchor on a reef just off Jamaica, when he lost his footing and fell into the water. Because it was so rough, he fell into the shallows between two huge waves. There wasn't enough water to break his fall, so he hit the coral hard."

"Ouch," said Jeffry. "That's gotta hurt."

"Yeah," said Bear. "It sure does." She had given herself a nasty scrape on some coral a few months earlier, and it had hurt a lot.

"So what happened?" Jeffry asked. "I mean, in your version."

"It's not just my version," I said. "It's what Daddy told me. The coral ripped his ankle bone right off his foot. The Jamaican doctors spent the next couple of days picking coral from the bone. Gangrene did set in, but Dad's good friend Dr. Leonard Dourmashkin flew down from New York with a high dose of antibiotics. That's what saved his foot. Or at least, that's what I was told."

"I don't know," Jeff said. "I think I like the other story better."

Pookie woke up and said, "Coo–ah," her favorite word, as if she was agreeing with her father. I picked her up and cradled her in my arms, then looked up to see Jeff and Bear watching me impatiently.

"Well, which was it?" Bear demanded. "The coral or the big lizard?"

I shook my head. I didn't know what to think. Just when

I thought I was getting somewhere, too. "I don't know, honey. The big lizard is kind of hard to believe, isn't it?"

"No," said Bear loyally.

"Did your father ever go to the Far East?" Jeff asked.

"Not that I know of. But we know he wrote for men's adventure magazines. He always used a pen name, and after a couple of stories he'd change to a new pen name—long live Marvin Schmeckabier."

"Why did he change his name?" Bear asked.

"I think he believed his work was good enough to stand on its own. He was doing his best not to compete with his brother. Writing with the Hemingway name is tough."

"So is writing without it," Jeff said.

"You know what I mean," I said. "There are always comparisons to Ernest. And damned few writers can stand up to that. And if it's your brother—or your father, for that matter— I can't imagine how hard it was. Ernest's son Jack—your cousin Mariel's dad, Bear—sent me a letter after Daddy died. I must've read it a hundred times. He said Daddy was a fine writer, and all the comparisons with his brother had hurt. But where fame and success killed some of the finest qualities in Papa, Daddy stayed unspoiled."

"What did he mean, unspoiled?" Bear asked.

"He meant, he liked your grandpa a lot," Jeff answered. "Most people did—and not just because he told good stories, but because he was a good guy."

I said, "When brothers or sisters grow up doing the same job, they tend to be competitive, or jealous. Your grandpa wasn't like that. I never heard him say one bad word about his brother." I leaned closer to Bear, and added, "You remember this now that you have a sister."

"I will." Bear nodded, and gave a little tickle to Pookie. Then she paused and looked at Jeff and me. "Will we ever find out if these stories are true?"

"We can try," Jeff said. He turned to me. "Did you ever see any souvenirs from the Far East? Anything that might be connected to this story? Giant lizard teeth, dragon skins, anything like that?"

"No, not unless—he had some really strange boots in the closet. I don't think he ever wore them. But they weren't snake or 'gator. I never asked."

"I want to hear the rest," Bear demanded.

"Okay, okay." Jeff said, and pushed the Play button. There was some clattering I couldn't identify in the background of the tape. Then the professor's voice came on.

"Sorry, Les. Very clumsy tonight."

"Can't hold his liquor," I heard Charlie Willeford say.

"Not with that hand," Dad answered, and they both chuckled.

"Here's a towel," my mother said.

"Thank you. Awfully sorry."

"There," my mother said, and there was a round of rustling, throat-clearing, and then once again the clink of ice into a glass.

"Where was I?" Daddy said.

"You were speaking of the emotional turmoil," the professor said.

"So I was."

"Well, ah—what emotional turmoil was that?"

"Well, ever since my first hunting trip with Ernest, I had believed my brother could get me out of the hardest of jams. No matter how bad things got, he would be there to pull me out of the soup. I think he believed this, too, and we had both just had a nasty reminder that it wasn't so. It shook us both up, and so on the way home, I got a good chewing out over every little thing I had done wrong on the trip, and in my life. It was a very long trip home."

"Didn't Ernest feel that after your father died, as eldest son, he was now in control of the family?"

"Absolutely, and he was. He helped me and my sisters, Carol and Sunny, financially."

"He was most tough on Carol, wasn't he?"

"Yes—she met John Gardner very young. Ernest was worried because John didn't have many business prospects, and forbade Carol to marry him. Carol didn't listen and they stayed married for more than fifty years. A great achievement considering how the rest of us turned out."

"So Ernest misjudged John Gardner?"

"Yes, absolutely. But Papa was just trying to look out for us. Look, this has nothing to do with hunting. Stick to hunting questions."

"Ahhh, I'm sorry. You said, since your first hunting trip with Ernest, you felt your brother could get you out of any jam. What happened on that first trip to make you believe that?"

"Hell, man, it wasn't just the first trip. Papa really did save my ass, more than once. Not just me, either. That's the kind of guy he was. He always seemed to know what the right thing to do was. And he didn't have a lot of doubt about whether he could do it. Wherever he was, he accepted responsibility."

"But for you," the professor insisted. "Didn't you say that this really started on your first hunting trip?"

I heard Daddy sigh deeply and take a drink. I was surprised to hear him answering all of the professor's questions so readily, and waited curiously to hear what he'd say. "Yes. I guess it did." Then he chuckled, and the chuckle turned into one of Daddy's big, booming laughs. "By God, I sure as hell won't forget that soon."

"Oh, dear, is this the one about the bear?" my mother asked.

My daughter nudged me, her face alive with delight. "The bear, Mommy," she said. "It's the bear story."

I smiled and squeezed her hand.

"A bear? You hunted a bear with Ernest?" the professor asked. "I've never heard anything about that."

"You wouldn't have," Daddy said. "I was only twelve. Our family had gone up to the summer place."

"You mean Lake Walloon?"

"Yes. Papa was visiting and decided it was time I learned to hunt. He showed me how to lay out a trap line, and every day I would go check the traps. But something went wrong right away. The traps would be sprung, but empty. I might find a few small shreds of an animal, but not enough to bring home. So Papa and I took a hike along the lake. We had gone maybe seven miles when we reached our trap line."

"What were you after?"

"Mostly small game. Things you can eat. It's a family law, as far back as I can remember: If you kill it, you eat it. So the traps were set for the edible varmints. Guess that's what got the attention of the old he-bear. I don't think I've ever been so frightened in my life."

"IT *IS* THE BEAR STORY!" my daughter interrupted, and Jeffry stopped the tape.

"It sounds like it," I said.

"Gee, honey," Jeffry said. "That's not what interested me. 'If you kill it, you eat it.' Now that's interesting. Where have I heard that before?"

"Don't go there," I warned him.

"What?" Bear said, sensing from our grins that something was up. "What is it?" She looked back and forth between Jeff and me.

"Ask your mom," Jeff said. "Before you hurt your neck."

"Mom?"

I laughed. "All right. You might as well know. I got my first BB gun when I was seven years old—"

"I'm seven," Bear said. "Can I have a BB gun?"

"We'll see. But if you get one, you get the same rules. Just like my father gave them to me."

"If you kill it, you eat it," Jeffry laughed.

"That's right," I said.

"That is *so* gross," said Bear.

"And so is eating frog and pigeon stew," said Jeffry.

"What? Mom, what is he saying?"

I had to laugh, too, remembering that day out behind our big old house on Miami Beach. "I had that BB gun about two days. Daddy had told me to be careful, never point it at something you weren't going to shoot, never point it at a person, always shoot away from the house—and—"

Jeff and Bear joined in and we all said together, "If you kill it, you eat it."

"That's right. I didn't have a problem with the other rules. But I didn't really believe him about that one. So I was out in the back yard with my BB gun, and I wanted to prove what a great hunter I was. I shot a pigeon from the sea wall, and I shot a frog over by the pond. And then I looked up to see Daddy. He was standing on the terrace with his arms folded, watching me. 'Nice shooting, daughter,' he said. 'Bring them over here.' I took the two little bodies over to him, and he looked at them. 'Two clean kills,' he said. 'Let's take 'em in to Mom.' So I carried them into the kitchen. I still didn't know what he was doing, until he called out to Mom that I was ready for my lunch and would she help cook."

"*Eeeeewwww*," said Bear. "No way!"

I smiled. "Way. Mom knew it was coming and she had the pot ready. And I had frog and pigeon stew for lunch."

"Mom!" said Bear with a horrified face. "You ate a frog?!"

"Some of it," I admitted. "That was the rule."

"It still is the rule," Jeffry said. "Are you sure you want a BB gun?"

"Yeah," said Bear. "But I'm not gonna shoot any frogs."

Jeff and I laughed. And I remembered fondly how Daddy had stood beside me that long gone day, watching me eat, and making sure I did. "A gun is a powerful tool, Hillsides," he had said. "Always use it properly. Remember that."

"I'll remember," I said, gagging on a bite of pigeon. And I did.

"So does your daddy eat the bear?" my daughter wanted to know. "Or does it eat him?"

I laughed again. "I don't know," I said. "Let's find out." I wound the tape back slightly and pushed Play.

"If you kill it, you eat it," Daddy was saying. "So the traps were set for the edible varmints. Guess that's what got the attention of the old he-bear. I don't think I've ever been so frightened in my life."

"Tell us about it, please, Les," the professor urged.

Dad paused and we could hear him take another sip of his drink. Then he began again.

THIRTEEN

MOST OF US know the feeling of having a dinner guest who just won't leave. Well, that's how it was with this bear. He had invited himself to our trap line and wouldn't back off no matter how bluntly we withdrew the invitation. So early this one morning Papa said, "It's no use, Baron. We've got to track and kill the bear."

I was only twelve years old. I had hunted plenty, but only small animals, like raccoons and birds. The thought of coming up against a nine-hundred-pound bear put real terror into me. On the way out I asked, "Can't we just poison him?"

Papa laughed, then shook his head and laughed again. He was twenty-eight, and I wanted him to be proud of his little brother. I never told him I wasn't kidding, but hell, we didn't have any poison, and anyway we both knew that wasn't the right way to do it. The animal suffered too much with poison, and whatever some people might say, Papa didn't want that. We were raised to believe that was wrong. So Papa suggested we build some bait piles to draw him in.

You do this by digging out a four-by-five-foot section of earth, only a couple of inches deep, and then you cover it with deadfall. That's trees that are dead, or have fallen to the ground. The deadfall protects the bait from smaller animals. Our bait was a bag of day-old doughnuts. Then to ring the dinner bell, Papa covered the doughnuts with licorice, sweet anise, and molasses. This should have brought the old he-bear running. But Moccasin Joe, as Papa called him, was just too smart. We sat in our blind and watched, and didn't see anything but squirrels. After a day and a night we decided to return to our cottage.

On the way back, Papa found Joe's tracks in the sand by the lake. "Look, Baron." He spread his hand across the imprint of Joe's hind foot. "This old he-bear has an eleven-inch paw. I'll bet he's a good seven foot tall."

Now I knew Papa was six-foot-four, so I tried to picture a bear that could stand bigger than him. One problem with being twelve and just under five foot is that you can easily picture such a beast, and it's never pretty.

Joe, we were about to learn, was about as big, shrewd, and shifty as an old bear can get. Papa figured he'd learned his tricks by robbing trappers up in Canada. Somehow he had made his way south to our part of Michigan.

When we returned to our cottage, Papa and I discussed the bear. The two times we'd caught sight of him, Joe had always seemed to know we were close, and had moved ahead or to one side with remarkable finesse. There was something almost supernatural about this bear.

And so I hadn't slept well the night before. I'd had confusing dreams of vanishing bears, and bears that had inherited the spirits of departed Indian warriors who delighted in harrying palefaces like those who'd robbed their brothers of their land centuries earlier.

I was envisioning old Moccasin Joe brushing against a huge bear totem pole and knocking it over with ease, when suddenly I was wide awake. It was still dark, but when I looked out our cabin window I could tell morning was near by the way Orion had shifted into the west against the high peaks out there.

Then I heard it again. I hadn't known what woke me, but hearing that faint sound convinced me I'd just heard the bear. It was a *sniffff,* a sort of long, drawn-in breath.

Then there was the lightest pressure against our door. My eyes adjusted to the darkness and I could see Papa was already up, rifle in hand. But when he swung open the door, the bear was gone.

It was another two hours before I finally dozed off again. When I awoke, Papa was up and had bacon and beans heating in a pan.

"You see anything last night?" I asked him.

"Not a thing. But outside, there's bear tracks all around. The front paws have claw marks four inches ahead of the pugs."

"So it was Moccasin Joe."

"In person. If we hurry and eat, we can track him from here. I don't think he's too far."

The trail led away, toward our trap line and bait pile. Papa didn't want to chance missing the old robber, so we didn't take any shortcuts and stayed to his trail.

Half a mile away we saw where Joe had stopped and tried to dig a family of ground squirrels out of their burrow. He'd just smelled them, but hadn't gotten any. At least, we didn't find any loose fur, and I saw two squirrels running around outside in the early-morning light. We followed Joe's tracks as they led up the side of a rock-slide, well above the lake.

"Let's just have a look-see," Papa said. "This is your day, kid. You're going to leap from beginner to big game. The trick here is not to get eaten."

"I'll do my best," I said, and then added, "Think we'll catch up with him today?" For a second I lost my footing and Papa reached out and grabbed my hand.

"Easy there. Look, relax a little. Even old bears make mistakes. His biggest was getting involved with us."

We reached the top and hurried on along the trail. Finally we came to the little bog where a creek had been almost filled with downed pines. Our trap line was just beyond.

"Come on, Baron. We're not waiting for him to hibernate. Let's put him to sleep for good."

"Agreed," I said, fighting the butterflies in my stomach. Old Joe had become a personal enemy. He'd crossed the line when he began haunting my dreams and making my waking hours miserable with fear. Then it dawned on me: fear was normal. It was even good. It kept you more alert. Everything seemed clearer. Sight, sound, and smell.

Papa suddenly stopped. He motioned for me to freeze. He pointed to the thicket of alders ahead of a patch of muskeg. "There."

I saw the bear then, too.

Even through the branches he looked huge, bigger than life. He was more like the bear that had been in my dreams than like any real animal. My mouth went dry just looking at him, and I wanted to wake up so he would go away, but I was already awake, and that huge old he-bear was not going anywhere.

Papa inched back to me and whispered, "I'm going to sneak around on the side. He doesn't know we're here yet, and with the breeze off the lake, he may not get wind of us until I'm close enough. Baron, you should have first shot. You've got real shocking power there." He pointed at my rifle.

I wanted to hand him back the gun, but instead I just nodded. I'm not sure I could have said anything, the way my tongue was sticking to the roof of my mouth. We both watched for a moment, then to make sure I understood, I asked. "I'll wait five minutes, then move to get a clean shot? Is he at the bait pile?"

Papa nodded. "Don't rush it, wait a full ten minutes. That is a very big bear, and a smart one. We've got to play this just right." And he moved off and was soon out of sight.

You asked me when I started to think that my brother could always save my hide, and I guess I was thinking it that day or I would have turned tail and run back to the cabin. Those few minutes while I sat there alone and waited for Papa to get into position seemed longer than a weekend in New York. I kept my eyes on where I knew the bear was and listened to my heart thumping, and I think the only reason I stayed was because Papa expected me to, and because I knew he was there if it started to go wrong.

So after what seemed a good interval, I took a deep breath, wiped my sweaty palms off on my pants, and stepped down toward the creek. But as I stepped, the rock under my foot gave way. I came sliding down to the water's edge.

I crouched there at the bank of the creek and felt the water trickling into one boot. Nothing seemed terribly wrong. The fall I'd taken seemed lucky now. I had more cover than Papa, who was working around to the other side. When he was in position, he would signal me and we would close in on our unlucky bear. Then I caught sight of the black bulk in the alder thicket fifty yards ahead. A little closer and I would have a clean shot.

My eyes moved back down to my rifle barrel. There was mud on the last three inches. My heart hammered. If what I suspected was true, I knew that missing my footing on the edge of this creek might have just cost me my life.

Papa was too far away to signal without the bear becoming aware of both of us. He would no doubt be mad as hell if he saw my gun. If our father had taught us anything, it was to take good care of hunting rifles.

I pulled the Springfield back with my right hand, wiped the muzzle with my left. With my clean hand I upended the rifle to make absolutely certain. There, where a .30-caliber hole should have been, a plug of mud filled the bore. Ah, hell, I thought. We're dead.

I was disarmed. Helpless. The rifle would explode if I fired without cleaning out the mud first. I had no knife and Papa's wouldn't do me any good. And less than fifty yards away, old Moccasin Joe, the massive black bear, clawed at our bait. With my rifle plugged with mud, I felt as helpless as a trapped animal.

Within minutes Papa would be close enough for the bear to smell him. Then the old he-bear would probably back off and head for me. Together we would have been a fair match for him. Papa was to hold his fire and back me up. This was how he had explained it, and if you knew him, you knew you had to do as Papa told you.

Why had he given me first shot? Perhaps it was to see if his little brother had it in him. See what I'd do when the bear charged. Of course, he added to the thrill when he warned me, "Old Joe there has the stuff to make hash out of both of us. Don't miss, Baron!"

Now, blast it, I had to get the mud out of my gun if I was ever to warm myself over a campfire again, not to mention stay in Papa's good graces. Which in itself was no easy trick. If I only had a cleaning rod. But I hadn't. Nor was there any sapling nearby that might reach the length of the barrel. There were alders up where the bear was, but I was damned if I was going to walk up to the bear with a useless gun and bat him on the head.

Carefully, my eyes on the bear, I crouched lower. I had one slim chance—better than doing nothing, but not by much. Slowly, ever so slowly, I eased the bolt up, and then back. There was a small snick as the bolt came back, bringing the cartridge out of the chamber. I put my hand over this cartridge and pocketed it. I heard it click against something else. With both hands holding my gun near the center of balance, I brought it up and tried to blow through the barrel. All I got was an oily taste. The mud didn't blow out, and that was that.

I tried shaking the gun, still holding the bolt open. No dice. I saw a slight movement and looked up at the bear. He might be scenting Papa already. I had only moments before I needed this rifle to save my life, and here it was, useless in my hands.

Remember, I was only twelve years old. My heart was racing. I looked at my gun, and then things began to click. I knew what my fingers had touched in my jacket pocket a moment before. It was a .22 long rifle cartridge, a single round for the pistol that was back at the cabin. But that single little missile might save me yet.

I lay the rifle down on the dry ground just ahead of me. My fingers dove for the little cartridge and found it. With my other hand I felt in my hip pocket for the length of fishing line I always carried for tying baits to the trigger pans of our steel traps.

Working with fingers that suddenly fumbled in their eagerness, I pulled the fishing line out until I had about a yard free. Then I made a slipknot at the very end and put the loop over the .22 cartridge. I pulled it tight and hefted it. It would do, if only I had time enough.

Carefully lifting the rifle again, I held it muzzle-down and eased the little cartridge into the breech. For an instant it turned sideways and I had to jiggle it with the line. I was afraid the line was too big, and would make it bind. Sweat poured down my face. Then the cartridge slid into the barrel and stopped.

I pulled on the fishing line again. This time it came most of the way up. I let go and the cartridge dropped with a little *thunk*. Holding the rifle higher, I looked at the muzzle. The mud plug protruded about a quarter of an inch; it was a start. A few more times and I'd be—

Ca-raaaak! It was Papa's .30–30. I couldn't see any movement where the bear had been, so I pulled down on the line again and let it go. *Thunk* went the little cartridge hitting the mud plug. Again I pulled on the line and let go. And again. Now the mud was out more than an inch.

I was just about to grab it and hope the whole thing would come out when a thrashing, crashing sound reached me over the murmur of the creek. I looked up and saw Papa break cover, running as I hadn't seen him run in years.

Wildly I pulled back on the string and let it fall, once, twice—

Then the bear burst through the brush, too, hot on Papa's trail. Papa made for me, until he was about twenty yards away. Then he saw the agonized look on my face, and the ridiculous way I held the gun, its butt toward the sky and its bolt open. He swerved and made for the nearest pines on my left.

The bear didn't seem to notice me. He was after Papa, and twice as fast. By the time Papa had gotten to the first trees, the bear was only a couple of loping bounds behind. I felt as angry and frustrated as a bee that's lost its stinger. I grabbed for the mud plug and it came away in my hand, but there was still more in the barrel.

Like an angel playing a harp with only one string, I plucked at that fishing line and heard the repeated little *thunk* within the barrel.

Papa whirled around the trunk of the first substantial pine, his rifle still in one hand. I could see that the lever was half-way open. The bear followed him growling and clawing.

I climbed out of the muskeg onto the dry ground, determined to do whatever I could even if it meant bashing the bear with my only weapon. Just then, the little .22 cartridge dropped out. The bore was clear!

As Papa came around the pines the second time, I could see he was just ahead of the bear and headed out at a dead run. Passing me, he yelled one word: "Shoot!"

I tugged the fishing line through, slammed in a fresh soft-nose cartridge, and closed the bolt. Swinging up on the old he-bear as he continued his charge, I pulled the trigger. *Boom!*

The bear reared up and I could see I had hit him hard in the shoulder. He was now twenty yards away and closing fast on me. There was no time to reload. I dropped the gun and ran back toward the pines.

I whipped around the first set of trees, and my foot caught a root that sent me sprawling. That was it; I knew my life was over. Only twelve years old, finished before I even started. I had time to feel really sad for myself for a split second. Then I looked up and forgot about everything but that bear. Old Joe rose up on his hind legs, panting, growling, deciding on his next move. Lucky for me, he didn't make a next move.

Boom! I heard my gun fire again and Joe's head shook. His right temple turned red. He swung back toward the field where the shot had rung out. There was Papa standing in the clearing. For a moment Old Joe stared across the clearing at Papa. Then he let out a heavy grunt and keeled over, five feet from me.

Papa ran over to me and held out a hand, and I stood. "What do you say we *never* do that again?" he said.

"Deal," I answered, and we shook on it. We both stood there and looked down at the huge old he-bear that had nearly had us for supper. Papa knelt beside the bear and marveled at its size and beauty.

"Hell of a bear to lose your cherry on." He laughed.

"Yeah." I felt the dry in my throat and swallowed a couple of times. I stood looking at old Joe with relief and sadness. I was sorry it had ended this way. The old he-bear was reduced to a large mound of fur, steaming in the fall air.

I touched my foot to the bear's forepaw, and to my relief, the bear didn't move. Somewhere above me I heard a blue jay call out.

"Why—" I started, "why did you fire that first shot?"

"Joe saw me," Papa answered. He ran his fingers through the fur along the bear's neck. "He came at me, and I hit him somewhere in the chest, but he wouldn't stop. I forgot to put my finger on the damned extractor, so it didn't work." He lifted the bear's lip above the gums and I saw the two-inch-long white teeth. "Damn, what a magnificent animal. Hey . . ." He turned and looked up at me. "What happened to you? What were you waiting for? An invitation?"

"Nope." I smiled. "I slipped and got the barrel plugged with mud. But I cleared it just in time."

"A few minutes earlier would have been better," my brother told me. "But at least you didn't panic." Papa stood up and looked at my shoulder. "What did you use to clear it?"

I pulled the .22 cartridge from my pocket, the string still on it, and handed it to Papa. He looked at it with a funny raised eyebrow.

"If I had known that's all you had—Jesus, Baron, you could have gotten us both killed. Good thing you got the old Hemingstein luck." Papa handed the cartridge back to me. "Keep it. If anything, it will remind you that your luck can always change."

It took us all day to skin out that old he-bear. I think Papa gave the pelt to one of his friends up in Horton Bay. They might still have it, I don't know.

FOURTEEN

GOOD LORD, if that had been my first hunt, it would also have been my last." The professor laughed.

"But it wasn't the last for Papa and Les," Willeford roared.

"No? What was?" the professor asked. There was the sound of pine needles crackling and I pictured my father adding fuel to his fire.

"Oh, something truly unusual," Willeford chuckled. "You'd never guess in a million years."

"Well, after all I've heard this evening, I can't imagine what sort of beast Les might consider unusual."

"Why, it wasn't a beast at all," my mother said. "It was Nazi U-boats." And I heard her shake her glass so the ice rattled.

"U-boats. Oh, yes, I heard about Papa's little 'crook factory' in Cuba. A hand-picked spy ring he used against the Nazis. Very romantic and exciting. Although Martha Gellhorn," the professor said slyly, "thought Papa's attempts to capture a U-boat were just an excuse to get extra gasoline rations for his daily fishing trips."

"No, Professor," my father finally rumbled. "Ernesto had real reason to believe Nazi U-boats were in the Caribbean. I know, because I brought him the proof."

"Proof?" the professor asked.

"Photos, charts with the locations. They were there."

"You're kidding. You gave him the idea of hunting Nazi U-boats?"

"What I said was I brought him the proof."

"Well, how did you—I mean, wouldn't someone, ah—?"

"Oh, for God's sake, just listen," Willeford answered.

It was January of 1940. There were rumors of German submarines between Key West and Cuba. President Roosevelt announced that an unidentified sub had been sighted off Miami; press reports from Trinidad told of a German mother-ship and three subs, and another five U-boats had been spotted in various areas of the Gulf. But America wasn't at war at this time, so it was a sort of see-no-evil, speak-no-evil deal. And you have to understand, too, that a lot of Americans hadn't made up their minds about this war. Most people thought it was none of our business.

Not Papa. In Spain he had seen firsthand what the Germans were up to, and he was going to do whatever he could to make damn sure they didn't do it to America. So in spite of America's neutrality and all the German promises to respect that, he believed the reports. He knew the Nazis were up to something in our coastal waters. But he also knew that Washington wouldn't do anything about it without some damned convincing proof.

Papa wasn't the only one who thought that way. He introduced me to an Englishman, Tony Jenkinson. Tony was a correspondent for the London *Daily Express.* He seemed to have money, and he even had a title he didn't use much. British Naval Intelligence had given him an assignment, and he needed a partner who could sail and wanted to do something adventurous.

If you knew me, this sounded too good to be true. After Papa got us together I talked with Tony a few times and we hit it off, and before too long I was looking for a boat, one of my favorite pastimes. We found and outfitted a lovely twelve-ton schooner, the *Blue Stream,* and headed out.

We were all pretty sure that there really were Nazi U-boats in the area, but finding one wouldn't be easy, and getting proof would be even harder. Tony and I hit on a scheme that we thought might work. A submarine in those days couldn't go very long without needing fuel, water, food, and so on. Instead of trying to find the U-boats, we would try to find their re-supply bases. They would be on land instead of underwater, and they wouldn't be moving around, and we decided they would be altogether a great deal easier to find.

We cruised for three months in the little-known waters of the western Caribbean. And not only did we find signs of a well-developed Nazi refueling system for submarines, we also saw preparations for German naval action off the coast of Central America and on remote islands near Mexico. In each location we discovered Nazi agents and Nazi propaganda, and huge stocks of diesel oil.

Now this was war, whether the U.S. was in it or not, and even then we knew that the Nazis didn't play by Marquess of Queensberry rules. They were writing a whole new rulebook for war, and one of the first rules was to shoot first and ask questions later. So how did we avoid getting ourselves killed? Not by being armed to the teeth—just the opposite. We did our damnedest to look innocent—and that meant no weapons and no backtracking.

We planned our route very carefully and stuck to the rules. International law requires a vessel to sail to its declared port without casual stopovers. But we knew the loophole to this law, which was to carry plenty of liquor on board to smooth the way with port officials, and always to have an "emergency excuse." We set up the boat with hidden tanks below the engine and could pump all our fresh water down to them. We drove a block of mahogany into one of the cylinders in an auxiliary engine. And so we were always out of water, or we could always have engine trouble when we needed it.

The first leg of the trip was as sweet as a baby's smile. The *Blue Stream* was the smoothest-sailing boat you could ever want, and we had a real vacation. We trolled a fishing line over the side, and the second day out Tony pulled in half of the biggest wahoo I have ever seen. The other half was taken by a huge hammerhead shark that came up out of the deep, sliced through that fish razor-clean, and just vanished. It made us think twice about dragging behind the boat on a rope, which we had been doing for the fun and to wash off the sweat.

In the Straits of Yucatán, a norther hit us. Those storms are always trouble. They come up fast, blow hard, and can last for days. We ran before the storm a day and a night. The sea whipped up some huge waves around us, and the *Blue Stream* climbed every monstrous wave and sliced the foaming crests like a hot blade through cream. She was a beautiful boat, and she gave us some wonderful rough-water sailing.

BEFORE I KNEW what I was doing, I had reached out and stopped the tape. Jeff looked at me with a worried frown. "What is it?" he asked.

"Nothing," I said. "This part of the tape. It just made me think of something."

"Something good?" Jeff asked.

"Yeah. I think so."

"Mommy," Bear interrupted. "Is a norther like a hurricane?"

"It's a big storm like a hurricane. With big waves and strong winds."

"So why wasn't Grandpa scared? He's in a hurricane and he sounds like he was having *fun*."

I smiled at her, the memories washing over me. "He was having fun, honey," I said. "Your grandpa loved adventures, and he loved sailing, and he knew boats. He always knew he'd be all right as long as he had a good boat under him."

"And that's what it made you think of," Jeff said.

I squeezed his hand. "Yeah," I said. "That's it."

And it was. I remembered the time I had been with Daddy in a similar storm, between Miami and Bimini. The waves were taller than the masthead, and each time a new gust of wind took us, or a big wave broke over us, he would laugh. He looked more alive laughing into the teeth of that storm than I had ever seen him before. I was thirteen then, and I finally said, "Daddy, are we going to be all right?" He laughed even harder and hugged me. "Don't sweat it, kid," he said.

I always remembered that: "Don't sweat it." When things got bad for me, that was my mantra. I would think of riding out the storm on that small sailboat with my father, and whatever else happened it didn't seem so bad. And I also realized that I had learned to enjoy whatever life might throw at me—"Don't sweat it." Keep smiling. Learn to love it. You might as well have fun whatever's happening, because life throws good and bad at you and all you can control is how you look at it.

That was Daddy.

And it was another small piece of the puzzle, too. Because that really *was* Daddy—the big, laughing man, with joy in his heart whatever life might bring him. A man who faced the storm with both legs on the deck.

And a man like that could never even think about life in a wheelchair. Losing both legs would have made him someone else, somebody he wasn't. It would have been a death more final and more painful than the one he chose, because it would have diminished who he was and made him somebody who was just surviving.

I pushed the Play button and listened as Daddy's voice rose up again.

After almost two days, the storm wasn't weakening, and we were starting to take on water. We'd already lost one sail—ripped out by the powerful winds, and we'd almost broached and sunk before I could get up a small storm staysail. And that damned norther showed no signs of blowing out. We needed to find a place to get our boat out of the wind. And on our second morning we sighted the island of Mujeres.

We took her around to the lee side of the island, out of the worst of the storm winds, and dropped anchor—only to discover that this sanctuary had a small Mexican naval station, with forty personnel and one gunboat.

We went ashore and introduced ourselves. They were polite, told us that of course we could stay until the storm blew out. We paid our respects to the commandant, a dapper little man wearing a custom-tailored uniform.

There's a way things work in Mexico, so we didn't go on shore empty-handed. And they didn't just take our gifts and send us back to the boat. After we made the commandant a few gifts of booze, money, and a Hawaiian shirt I had, we were given a tour of the island. He had been giving us the eye, and I could tell there was something he wanted to say, but he just took us around his little base, pointing out the scenic highlights: the big new wharf, the barracks, the radio tower. At last, as we looked at the power plant with its huge diesel engine, the commandant said, "It is German. They always make the best products. Far superior, in everything. Germany, of course, will win the war."

And the way he said it and then looked at us, it was clear to me. He said this to see our reaction. Tony cued me not to protest—not that I would have. I was the commandant's guest, and he could just as easily throw us in the brig and take our boat if he felt like being nasty. Besides, we were spies. I was aware that one of the requirements of the job is to know when to keep your mouth shut.

So we just nodded and agreed that it was a beautiful engine, and he seemed satisfied. It was my first taste of being a spy in another man's country.

But for the commandant of such an isolated base to have obvious Nazi sympathies was just the sort of thing we had been looking for. A man like that in place here would make this a great spot for a U-boat fuel dump, and Tony was sure there was one.

And just to nail that point down, later that night we rowed around the island taking depth readings and making notes. Swinging the lead from the rowboat in nearly complete darkness, we found an isolated spot just offshore that had been dredged to a depth of thirty-six feet. Tony knew the largest of the German subs needed thirty feet of depth to come in. We followed this deep channel and found that one end of it led out to the deep water of the Straits. The other end went right up to a newly built concrete shed on the shore.

Now, there was no one around on this island except the Mexican navy. The nearest land was miles away. And yet this shed was built like a bunker and locked up tight with the finest locks you could buy—German locks, just like the generator.

"I believe I smell a small rodent, Les," Tony said. "Shall we have a look?"

I admit I was nervous. If you got caught spying, it was the same thing anywhere—a bullet to the head. But after all, this was what we had come for. The navy base was on the far side of the island, and we would surely hear or see something if a U-boat came in. So I told him, "Lay on, Macduff," and he surprised me by pulling a lock-pick out of his pocket. I kept watch while he fiddled with the lock, and in just a couple of minutes he had the door open.

"What is it you colonials like to say?" Tony asked me. "Bongo?"

I turned and looked inside. "Bingo," I said. "A five-star bingo, Tony."

In the light of his small flashlight, which he insisted on calling a torch, we counted seven hundred drums of diesel fuel. That was thirty-five thousand gallons, enough to take one submarine twice around the Caribbean.

"That would run a generator for an awfully long time," I said. "Especially an efficient German generator."

"That it would," he agreed. We had struck paydirt the first time out. There was no question about it. Add seven hundred barrels of diesel fuel to the newly dredged channel and the pro-Nazi commandant, and the fuel could be there for only one reason—and it wasn't for the little gunboat.

With the light of Tony's "torch," I took as many photographs as I could, shooting the lock and the bunker, outside and in, and then we rowed back to the *Blue Stream*. Since we had known we'd be taking photographs, and since we didn't want to get shot for having them, we were ready with a hiding place. I put the spent film in a cigar box under the ship's head. That turned out to be a pretty good hiding place. We were searched twice on that trip, but no one ever found our stash.

The storm blew itself out early the next day. We hauled anchor and headed back out to sea just a few hours after dawn. I remember sitting in the cockpit with a mug of coffee and looking back at the Mexican base. A few of the sailors were out on the pier. They waved to us, and we waved back. Then we got the mainsail up and headed south.

Our next stop was Cozumel. Here we discovered another young Mexican who was ambitious, energetic, and very pro-Nazi. His name was César Rivera. César was the radio operator for an American company. He ran the radio from the second story of his bar. When we entered the bar we heard a metallic voice boom out, "This is Berlin calling! Our victorious troops struck another smashing blow at the enemy today."

After a few drinks, I went over and asked César, "So you really want Germany to win the war?"

"Of course," he answered. "Britain never did us any good. When Hitler wins he will bring order to the world."

Arguing the point with him would no doubt have shortened our trip. César kept a .45 strapped to his hip.

Of course there were some rough characters floating around the Caribbean back then—there still are. But the pistol seemed like overdoing it a little for an ordinary radio operator. Now, if you're also a link in the German supply chain, providing communications for the Nazis and blocking it for their enemies—why, then walking around with a big pistol strapped to your hip starts to make sense.

But there was no proof of anything like that, unless we could catch him in the act of passing information. And even if we did—his side had all the guns. We just had a sailboat and a camera. So I got him to stand beside the radio and smile while I took his picture—I told him it was for a magazine article on sailing the coast of Mexico. In fact, it went into a file that Tony handed in when we went home. We had no proof that César did anything, but we weren't in much doubt, either.

The next morning Tony and I set sail again. The trick to the spy business is always to keep moving. So we headed almost due south, looking for the next likely link in the Nazi chain.

Our hunches told us that somewhere in the neighborhood of Belize there would be another U-boat fuel dump, but our charts didn't show anything likely in the area. So we marked out a two-hundred-square-mile box and went through it systematically. On only the second leg of our search we found a small island that seemed perfect. It wasn't on the charts, which was a real advantage for a secret base. It had deep water on the lee side, which was another, so we decided it was worth a look.

But when we dropped our anchor in the small natural harbor, it turned out that our "deserted island" was far from deserted. An old steel trawler lay at anchor downwind from us. Its captain came out on deck and stared at us. He was wearing a battered captain's hat and the kind of clothes you might expect on the bridge of a tramp steamer, but he had a pistol on, too, and the way he stood and stared at us looked awfully military.

"There's one, or I'm an Arab," Tony said. And he called out, "Hullo!" and waved cheerily.

The captain didn't think much of that. He called back in a short, explosive answer: *"Geh weg!"*

That meant "Go away!"

As I said before, we were ready with a number of really good excuses. We were all set to tell him that our engine was kaput, and that we needed fresh water. But we weren't ready for what he did next.

As Tony called out a couple of phrases in deliberately awful German, the Captain pulled up his anchor and headed straight at us.

We were sitting there at anchor, sails furled and engine off. We never had a chance. I was sure he would shear off and just give us a scare, but he fooled me. He never wavered, just headed straight at us. I remember Tony yelling, "He's going to ram us," and then the awful shock as he hit. And that was it. Lights out.

When I came to, there was a dent on the cabin from where my head had slammed into the bulkhead, and a much bigger dent on the stern of the *Blue Stream*. Tony had pulled up the anchor, raised a sail, and got us under way before that crazy Kraut bastard could swing around and hit us again.

We left never knowing what the German was protecting on that island. But we sure as hell marked it in our report.

After that we sailed to Bonacca, a small island off British Honduras. We were told it was inhabited by descendants of seventeenth-century British buccaneers. Instead we found German music playing in the island shops, Nazi pamphlets in every store—and a real hatred of the British by the Spanish-speaking Bay Islanders. One of the shopkeepers even told us that Germans would make Honduras into the great country it was destined to be.

As we were leaving, we took a look around Bonacca's deep, sheltered harbor. You could put half a fleet in there and nobody would ever spot it. And tied to a dock was a German seaplane. I got a couple of good pictures and we hightailed it back to the *Blue Stream*.

But it seems that while we were nosing around, some of the island's inhabitants had been searching our vessel. There was nothing incriminating on board, not that they could find, anyway. I rushed right to our hiding place under the head, but they hadn't found it. The rolls of film were still there, untouched. We checked the whole boat carefully, but the only thing missing was a couple of bottles of booze.

We continued south and found a stronger Nazi base after

we rounded Nicaragua, and it seemed that the further we went, the more the whole thing came all the way out into the open. There were several islands in the area where we found barges dredging out lagoons. The guys working these barges were actually wearing their German uniforms. They made no attempt to disguise themselves or what they were doing. They were building German bases, and thanks to some pretty good propaganda and a lot of well-placed gifts, the locals were pretty much on their side.

Later, the locals told us that the Nazis had flown over the parts for prefabricated submarines. And on the next island over we learned that a British schooner, the *Alston,* had been sunk by a torpedo. Of course, the Brits were actually at war with Nazi Germany, and the U.S. was still neutral, so I wasn't worried too much about us. But still—for a U-boat to fire on a wooden sailing ship!

"Christ, Tony," I said when we heard about the *Alston.* "I'm sure glad as hell we're flying U.S. colors."

"For once, I am, too," he said. And we both really believed that the U.S. flag would keep us safe. But hell, remember this: This was the war that changed forever the way wars are fought. Things were just starting to heat up over there, and we weren't calling it World War Two just yet. So we still hoped we'd be all right. We weren't naive—that was just the way things had always been, and we didn't know yet that the Nazis had changed everything. A neutral flag didn't mean a hill of beans to them, and we were about to find that out the hard way.

Our next stop was a couple of islands at the mouth of the Panama Canal. The locals had told us of a large German ship supposedly fishing for sharks. We found her at anchor and looked her over. The only equipment we could see had nothing to do with fishing. She was outfitted to take depth soundings and land readings to make more current charts.

Finally we found what we were looking for off the coast of Costa Rica. In the lee of an outer island, we spotted not one, but two German U-boats tied up at the end of a long dock. They were huge, oceangoing-class boats, each with a two-story conning tower. Next to the *Blue Stream,* they seemed as big as battleships. We motored by within a hundred yards. Tony waved while I was down below noting their location on the chart and taking pictures through a porthole. We tried our best to look unconcerned, like locals. It must have worked, because they never took the cover off the big deck gun. We continued toward the harbor of Limón, feeling like champions who had just won a race. We had just found actual U-boats, and we had the documentation, and all we needed now was to restock our provisions to get safely home.

We wondered why the government of Costa Rica had not patrolled its coastline better, but we were about discover that Costa Rica wasn't even trying. Everyone in town was pro-

Nazi. The largest hotel in Limón was German-owned. It was like being in an outpost of the Greater Third Reich. We found ourselves trying to look more German, just to fit in. Shaving off the beards, tucking in the shirts, putting a little extra snap in the stride. We were sure it was working until our second day.

We entered a local market and found several men, including the owner of the market, listening intently to a German news broadcast from Berlin. The owner asked, "Why are you here?" He asked in English. So I answered him in English, "To buy some eggs."

"We have no eggs until tomorrow," he said.

"We'll be back then," Tony said in German.

"I don't think so. You are leaving tonight," he continued in English.

So I asked, "Why do you say that?"

"There are many reasons. But clearly the love of life is number one."

Tony and I had been seeing Nazis under every bush for the last few weeks, and now, when they had finally jumped out at us, we took it seriously. We hurried back to the *Blue Stream,* intending to get under way immediately. But the second we climbed on board our boat, we knew she had been searched again—a lot rougher this time. Bunks were pulled up, cushions heaved about. They had found one of Tony's notebooks, but not my film.

"Ahh, damn it, man," Tony yelled from our engine room. "Someone has monkeyed about with our electrical."

"Do you see any explosives?" I asked, passing him a flashlight.

When a solid search turned up nothing, Tony pulled the switch to crank over our engine. To our relief we didn't blow up.

"Guess we buggered their job before they could finish," Tony said, laughing. We left that very same hour, but as we came around a mangrove island and into the open water, breathing a sigh of relief at our narrow escape, we found it was even narrower than we had thought.

I was at the helm. Tony had just raised the jib when he spotted a U-boat on the surface. It was a thousand yards off our starboard bow. "Leicester," he called to me, and there was something in the quiet tone of his voice that made me snap to attention. "Tell me what you see there." He pointed to a patch of water between the U-boat and the *Blue Stream*.

I looked where he was pointing. For a moment I thought it might be a dolphin. They had been playing in the water around us for most of the trip. But this dolphin was moving awfully fast—and it was coming straight at our boat.

"Jesus Christ," I said.

"That's what I thought, too," Tony said. As he raced back toward the helm, I saw the U-boat picking up speed and bearing down on us.

Tony dove below and grabbed my film and his notes as I grabbed the line of the dinghy we were towing and pulled it alongside. I stood and looked at the dolphin. It was a hell of a lot closer now, and there was no longer any possible doubt.

It was a torpedo. The Nazi U-boat had fired at us, just like at the *Alston*. And we had only a few seconds before it hit.

"Tony!" I yelled at him. "Get up here *now*!" I jumped into the dinghy and he came racing up from below and over the side.

We only got four good pulls on the oars before the *Blue Stream* took a direct hit mid-ship. Her mahogany hull exploded in a flash of orange amid yellow-and-white sea spray. Broken planks and flaming debris rained down around us, but we kept rowing.

I know it isn't much when you think about what was about to happen over the next five years, but I was mad as hell at the Nazis. The *Blue Stream* was a beautiful boat, and to see her blown into toothpicks like that and know there wasn't one goddamned thing I could do about it—

And it wasn't over yet, either. The U-boat was a lot closer now, and it had opened fire on us with machine guns. I kept my head low and rowed as the machine gun fire raked the water's surface.

"I don't suppose you could row just a teensy bit faster, Les?" Tony asked me.

"No," I admitted, "but you're welcome to try."

A line of bullets stitched the side of the boat. We both ducked.

"Thanks awfully," Tony said from the bottom of the boat. "But you carry on."

We didn't really have any choices. It was clear that surrender wasn't on the Nazis' menu, so we did the only thing we could. We headed into the shallowest possible water so the U-boat couldn't follow us and then splashed ashore at the nearby mangrove finger and ran into the trees. The finger connected to the mainland through a sand bar. We never looked back.

I don't know if the U-boat sent a search party. Perhaps they figured we would be picked up in Limón. But we didn't go that way. Instead we headed south, toward the Panamanian border. After a week, we reached the coastal town of Guabito. There we were able to book safe passage back to Cuba.

"No way," Jeffry said, stopping the tape. "Blown out of the water by a Nazi torpedo?" He laughed. "And then slogging through the jungle for a week? What did they do for food? For water? That's some of the worst jungle in the hemisphere—the Green Berets train there."

"Da-aad!" said Bear. "Grandpa said it happened! Isn't it true, Mommy?"

"I don't know," I said. "A lot of it was true. I remember my mom saying he had written a story about it for *Reader's Digest*."

"Hey, there was an old copy of that in the box I picked through." Jeff said. "Hang on a second." He got up and went back to the hallway. I heard him sneeze, then say, "Gotcha." A moment later, he was standing in the doorway waving a small green-covered magazine. "November, 1940. 'Caribbean Snoop Cruise,' by L. Hemingway and A. Jenkinson. Son of a—gun," he said.

"Cool!" said T. L. Bear with a huge grin. "I told you they were true stories."

"We'll see," I said. I didn't want to burst her bubble. But I wasn't convinced.

Jeff started thumbing through the *Reader's Digest*. "It's all here," he said. "Just like on the tape."

"Dad, quiet," Bear said as she started the tape again.

There was a long silence on the tape. Then I heard the professor clearing his throat. "Yes, but Les—" he started, and then there was another pause.

"What?" my father asked.

"Well, er—nothing," the professor said.

"Nothing at all?"

Then I heard my mother laugh—a warm sound I already missed so much it hurt. "He doesn't get it, dear," my mother said. "He wants to ask what possible relevance your story has to Ernest and hunting."

Charlie Willeford laughed and said, "Yes, what were you hunting, Les? The innermost human psyche?" and the professor said, "Ah, well, actually, I mean—" and for a minute they were all talking at once.

"Is that it, Leech?" Daddy demanded. "You don't get it?"

"Well, you see, it's merely that—"

"It's all 'merely' with you, isn't it?"

"Perhaps so," he said. "But doesn't that make me a good audience for your stories?"

"Touché," my mother said softly.

After a long moment I heard my father chuckle. "All right, Herr Doktor Professor," Daddy said. "It is late, and we have all been drinking. So tell me. How can I bring you joy?"

"It was just, ah—you *did* say this was your last hunting trip with Ernest, and yet you end up torpedoed without really hunting anything and you hardly mention Ernest at all—"

"So you were listening," Daddy said.

"Well, yes, actually, I was, and—I mean, terrific adventure, very exciting, but—"

"But no Ernesto."

"And no hunting," the professor said. "Not really."

There was a short pause, then the sound of liquid pouring into a glass. "All right," said Daddy. "Fair enough." I heard him take a drink before he started to talk again. "The thing is, without my snoop cruise, Ernest would never have gone hunting U-boats himself. Now, I'm not trying to hog credit here, don't misunderstand. But the reaction I got in Washington made Papa mad as hell."

"Reaction?" the professor said. "But you had photographs, proof."

"That's right. We had proof. Pictures and notes on U-boats, locations of refueling stations. But that's all we had—proof. And that's never enough. Now, Tony—he returned to England a hero for his work. Me? I couldn't get Washington to acknowledge that there was any German danger at all."

"But that's madness," the professor said.

"No, that's politics. I must have done it wrong, or tried to talk to the wrong person. Remember, we weren't at war yet, and there were plenty of people in this country who thought the Germans had some pretty good ideas.

"Of course, Papa wasn't one of them. So he made some calls. And finally some fellows from the OSS came down to Cuba, collected my photos and notes—and to our surprise declared everything unreliable."

"Unreliable photographs," my mother murmured.

"It's the first rule of espionage; if you didn't do it—it doesn't count."

"And so Ernest got mad."

"Certainly, but I think he also thought of a sub hunt as patriotic. I know he gave me a lot of flack about only shooting with a camera. And he was sore as hell that I had lost the *Blue Stream*."

"And so he decided to get involved?"

"Well, for almost a year he got sidetracked looking for

German spies in Havana, but a year later a couple of local fishermen told of German U-boats surfacing alongside *viveros*—the local fishing boats—and stealing their catch. Then they'd go back to torpedoing freighters. By 1942, the U-boats were sinking one of our ships every four hours. So Papa came up with a plan."

"Did you help him?" the professor asked.

"Only on one of the trips," my mother answered, "and the Nazis weren't the only snakes in the waters."

"No?—I'm afraid I don't—"

"Listen. Even though I never said anything, my actions had challenged Papa to do better. I had photographed U-boats. So he decided he had to capture one."

"*Capture a U-boat?* With the *Pilar*? You're joking."

"I am not."

"But that's crazy."

"You don't have to tell me that, Professor. I was there."

FIFTEEN

Papa called it Operation Friendless. He named it after one of his cats, a lucky one who had beaten the odds after getting roughed up by a pack of dogs. That's how Papa felt about Nazi sub-hunting. He was the lone lion going out to prowl for German sea wolves.

On board the *Pilar,* he stashed three machine guns, two bazookas, a box of hand grenades, and a home-made bomb. The bomb was a box-shaped thing with hand-grips welded to the sides for better flinging ability. Papa kidded that he wasn't going to dance with the Krauts, he was going to have a *fling.*

And if the bomb was flung just right, the three pounds of gun-powder would be triggered by the four attached grenades, and it would blow a grand hole in the conning tower.

Among Papa's crew, he had hand-picked a couple of Cuban pelota players, Patche and his pal, Julius. Both were big men. Two weeks before I had arrived, Papa had taken the boys out to practice. They lobbed a dozen grenades on the reef off Cay Sal. Papa told me later the water had turned white from so many fish popping to the surface. He collected over two hundred pounds of snapper and grouper and gave it to the island poor.

By 1943, it was well known that German subs were work-ing off Florida and around Cuba. One morning Papa invited three of the local fishermen to his house for lunch. The Finca Vigía was the name of Ernesto's hilltop home in Cuba. I had arrived from Key West for a week's visit and Ernest had invited me to stay at the guest house. He asked that I come meet these fishermen.

When I entered the living room, I found that several oth-ers had also joined the meeting. The *Pilar*'s captain, Gregorio Fuentes, was there, and a taller man who turned out to be Winston Churchill's cousin, Winston Guest. Ernest's sons were not there. Patrick—Mouse, as Papa called him—had already left for boarding school, and Gregory, or Gigi, was down the hill playing with Gregorio's kids. Of course, most of the con-versation was in Spanish and it was thirty years ago, but here's what I remember.

Papa asked the fishermen to describe their encounters with the U-boats—or U-boat. It was important to find out if there was more than one working the area. Papa also wanted to know what was similar in the way they boarded the *viveros,* or what was different. He said it would help to get into the head of the German commander. He then questioned each man on specific details. He was trying to get an accurate reading of the true size of the sub or subs. How high the conning tower stood off the water surface—could they see the width of the hatch? If his plan was to work, he needed to know. He spent about three hours talking to the fishermen. And when he put all their stories together he was convinced it was all one sub, and based on that he came up with a plan.

I have to admit the plan was simple. Papa would keep nosing the *Pilar* around until they picked up the sub. He was sure that if he got close, the U-boat would surface and order the *Pilar* alongside as it had done with the other fishing boats. But the *Pilar* would be ready.

Patche and his pal would arm the bomb, as Papa brought the *Pilar* abreast of the sub's conning tower. Then the pelota players would fling the bomb over the tower's lip. The rest of us would open up with bursts of machine-gun fire to keep the Krauts from reaching the deck gun. The bomb would then either blow the watertight hatch off, or fall below and explode the periscope control area. Either way, we'd have a sub that couldn't dive. Papa figured then to grab her code books and armament, and to take the crew as prisoners.

Up until this meeting, I thought Winston Guest was nothing more than an English playboy. Unlike Tony Jenkinson, Guest did not have an intelligence assignment. But after the interviews, Guest surprised me and was able to identify the U-boat. It turns out it was a class-740 oceangoing attack sub. At a hundred eighty feet long, with three diesels, this sub had a surface cruising speed of twenty knots. The chance of Papa's thirty-eight-foot *Pilar* with its relatively weak twin screws catching this sub seemed pretty slim.

But Papa was confident that if he could raise one, he could complete the mission. The success rested on the height of the conning tower. If the ballast was blown and the sub had less than half its fuel, the tower would stand over thirty feet high. The pelota players would not be able to fling the bomb to the tower's deck. The fishermen were unable to agree on the conning tower's height because at sea, it was hard to gauge height. Their limited description was that the tower seemed about the same height as the seagoing tug that ran barges out of Key West. That gave Papa hope, since he knew that this tug had a height of only twenty feet.

The *Pilar's* captain, Fuentes, was not so eager to engage the U-boat. He wanted to know if Germans had ever fired on fishing boats.

"No," the tallest of the three answered. "They didn't even take the cover off their big deck gun. All they wanted was food. They took our entire catch, plus whatever else we had on board—chicken, bread, fruit."

"This is perfect, isn't it, Baron?" Papa grinned. "We'll go as decoys, offer them the catch. Then when their guard is down we let them have it."

A few days after this meeting, Fuentes returned to the Finca. "Papa," he said, "I don't feel so good about meeting submarines without some armor for the boat."

"Okay," Papa agreed. "Go see what you can find at the Havana boatyard."

That week, the *Pilar* had four quarter-inch steel sheets laid up against her hull. On the bow section, a full one-inch-thick sheet was fashioned. It gave the *Pilar* ramming capabilities and the ability to deflect anything but a five-inch gun, and maybe even that. But after two days of cruising with the armor, Captain Fuentes said, "Papa, I don't sleep so well with armor on the side. We are too slow in the water."

"Yes," Papa agreed. "She cuts the waves like a water-soaked log."

A day later, the dock workers removed all the special steel plates.

One evening a navy officer called Papa from Washington to ask how things were going. He kidded Papa and asked how he planned to entertain the Führer when the German commander took him and his crew back to Berlin.

"I'll sit in my cell and write dirty limericks for the Kraut bastards. But the biggest joke will be on you and our navy. Because you failed to give our crew a fighting chance."

A week later, Papa received $32,000 worth of RDF, or radio direction finder, equipment from the U.S. Navy. It took up most of the forward cabin. But Papa now had a better chance of hunting down a sub, instead of waiting for one to surface for air.

I only joined this group for one hunt. I'm not going to lie and tell you we got our sub that night, because we didn't. But we did locate a U-boat that had run aground. We used that fancy RDF equipment to get a triangular fix.

In truth it was the end of a perfect day. We had been out since first light, listening and fishing. Fishing was something Papa took seriously and that was because there is a hell of a lot more to it than just catching the fish.

Just two months earlier, Papa had taken several ichthyologists from the Philadelphia Academy of Science out fishing to catalogue the various marlin species in the Gulf Stream. One of the species caught was actually named after Papa, *Neomarinthe hemingwayi*.

From that point on, Papa kept records on all the fish he caught. At what depth, bait used, species, size, weight, and water temperature. This later became the goal of a group called the International Game Fish Association, an organization Ernest founded with his friend Mike Learner. But instead of working with Philadelphia scientists, the IGFA formed a relationship with the American Museum of Natural History.

It was after releasing a beauty of a sailfish that Sir Winston heard the distress call from the German U-boat. He and Papa got the fix of their location—just off the Cayo Confites reef. There were only six of us on board—Papa, myself, Winston, the two pelota players, and Captain Fuentes.

By the time we reached the island, the sun was already setting. I truly expected to see the silhouette of a U-boat against the last of the golden sunset, but instead we found nothing. Papa told Fuentes to circle around to the other side and follow the edge of the reef until it dropped off into the Gulf Stream. We moved slowly and carefully along the edge, peering down into the crystal-clear water. But after almost an hour, we had found nothing. The U-boat was gone and now so was our light.

"We need to know which way it's headed," Papa called over the churning of the *Pilar*'s motors.

"Maybe it's not gone. Maybe it's taking aim at us right now," Fuentes said in Spanish. "It's not safe to hunt the sons of whores in the dark."

"Grow some balls, man," Papa countered, also in Spanish. "Baron, get the mask and fins from under the forward bunk.

You're going for a swim. Winston—crank up the underwater floodlight. I want to find where that fornicating illegitimate went aground. Then we can figure which way it was heading, and give chase."

I slipped below and got the gear. The fins were old and since rubber was scarce, we were lucky to have them. Just my luck, they fit. I was hoping to give this job to one of the pelota players. Instead, I pulled my shirt off, sat the mask on my head, and slipped my feet into the black fins.

The stars were coming out from behind the clouds when I came out on deck. Fuentes had cut the engines and the *Pilar* was riding at anchor, swaying gently in an easy sea. Winston held the heavy, insulated floodlight while Patche and Julius hand-cranked the three-kilowatt generator into life. It had been saved from a fire that had burned down most of a movie theater in downtown Havana. Now it powered both my air regulator and the floodlight. I hooked the light onto a foot-wide insulated plate on the front of my belt. There were two hundred feet of wiring and hose that connected me to the boat. The electric wire had been specially coated to be waterproofed, but Winston still gave me a word of warning. "Careful, old chum. Salt water is an especially good conductor."

"I'd hate to be mistaken for an electric eel," I answered. To tell the truth, I had an almost superstitious fear of mixing electricity and salt water. I knew it was mostly nonsense, but I didn't like it. Still, it wasn't the kind of thing you talked about, so I didn't. Instead, I looked over the side. On the surface of the water, the half moon's reflection danced on the waves. Looking down into the dark depths I saw no movement.

Fuentes returned from setting the anchor. "Maybe we give the Germans something to shoot at, eh? Like a Christmas tree on the ocean." He flipped on a switch under the console and the spotlight that hung from the flying bridge snapped on. The aft deck became bright as day and the water off the stern a rich blue-black.

"Good luck, Baron," Papa called out to me. I saw he had pulled out his faithful tommy gun. The last time I had seen that gun I was returning from freeing the *Pilar*'s anchor, and Papa had persuaded a twelve-foot hammerhead not to eat me. He'd put six slugs into that queer-shaped head, and finally the beast sank in a stream of red.

I tried not to think about that shark, or about his many cousins. Nor of my fear of electricity and water. I just held my breath and flipped over the side into the water. The warm darkness swallowed me. I turned upright and sank to the bottom.

SIXTEEN

THE MUSCLES of my mouth tightened and the pressure from the water pushed in at my lungs. I had to suck hard to get a breath through the hose. Finally my flippers came to rest on the reef. It was darker than midnight in a coal cellar, but I hesitated to switch the light on. I imagined I could feel the electricity jolting up my arm and frying me into bacon rinds.

But hell, I was here to do something, and it was now or never. I leaned over and snapped on my light. My stomach knotted anticipating the shock, but instead the floodlight came on. All was fine.

The light made a widening tunnel straight ahead. It was pale yellow, fading out into the surrounding blackness. About fifty feet away I found a school of groupers snoozing. Startled by the light, they quickly swam off. I focused my light at ten feet, although my flood blurred out to thirty or forty feet. It was beautiful down there.

I kicked out to swim and found that the trailing hose, wire, and equipment made me as awkward as a pregnant pig. I came around a large coral head and discovered a whole school of butterfly fish swaying in the reef's wash. They were the usual vivid yellow-and-black and did not seem to mind the light, circling around in as much as out of the beam. I made another ninety-degree turn and at the end of the light I saw a giant fish. I didn't get a really good look, but I figured it measured about eight feet. It may have been a sailfish, since we were right at the edge of the reef. And it might have been something else, something I didn't want to think about too much. The place where the reef meets the big water is a feeding ground for all kinds of things, especially at night.

But whatever it was, it shot out of sight like the proverbial bat, and since I had only two hundred feet of wire and hose, I could not have gone after it even if I had wanted to—which I did not. I was not down here to chase fish. I was here to find a clue to the direction the U-boat had been heading when it ran aground.

When I got to the end of my lifeline I turned and worked my way back diagonally. There were two heads of coral blocking my path. They rose from the bottom to within three feet of the surface, then dropped again on the other side. I had to be careful not to get my lines tangled in their sharp edges.

As I came up and over the living rock, a giant trunkback turtle swam by me. I froze and watched the seven–foot giant pass. I wondered why she wasn't on the surface at this time of night, then shrugged it off. Probably the vibration of the *Pilar's* engines or the hum of the generator. But when I came over the coral ridge I saw the true reason. I had found what we were looking for.

The reef had been crushed to a milky white cloud. Mangled plants and a few pieces of fish littered the scene. This whole section of the reef resembled a broccoli patch that had been chewed up by a giant lawn mower.

This was clearly the spot where the U–boat had run aground. I swam through the white water, trying to see which way the sub had been heading when it grounded. But my flood light only added to the cloudiness. I held my hand up; I could just barely make out my fingers only inches from my mask. I turned off the light and swam slowly ahead.

I counted each kick and tried to figure out how far across the breach in the rock was—and after twenty-five kicks, I found the other side. Knowing both sides, all I had to do was point my hand compass toward the reef's shallowest point to get the sub's compass heading on grounding. I surfaced and saw the breakwater.

In the moonlight, the needle swung to a heading and then steadied. *Got you, you Kraut bastard—north by northwest.* About seventy-five feet away, the *Pilar* rocked slowly in the ocean's swells. I could hear the low tones in Spanish as the two pelota players placed bets on my success. Patche was from the hill country; he didn't like the idea of being in the water at night. Julius was talking him into a bet of ten dollars American that I would not make it back to the boat.

I sank back beneath the waves, smiling, and swam toward my brother's boat. When I cleared the two big coral heads, I dropped to a depth of twenty feet. I flipped on the floodlight again and made my way back along the reef.

I had gotten Papa his answer. All seemed right with the world. I was even enjoying this slow swim back. The undamaged areas of the reef were beautiful—and when my spotlight picked out some clump of brightly colored life, the surrounding darkness made the colors seem that much more startling and bright.

Several minutes passed while I continued toward the *Pilar.* I noticed what I thought were occasional needlefish moving overhead and thought nothing of it. But my indescribable peace was suddenly broken by three sharp tugs to my floodlight's wire. What followed surprised me even more—the muffled sound of the tommy gun's rattle and the much closer sound of the slugs hitting the water right above me, *ploit, ploit, ploit, ploit, ploit, ploit, ploit.*

I could only think of one reason why Papa might be shooting when I was in the water. I looked for sharks—and saw none. As far as I could tell, there was no reason for any shooting, unless they were just plain bored waiting for me. They certainly had no good reason to shoot at the handful of needlefish in the water. I was annoyed at their impatience—they were endangering me with their recklessness—but I picked up my pace. There was no sense me staying down here if they wanted to shoot. It sure seemed like bad timing.

There was another hard tug on my line, and I realized they were pulling me in. *Hey, calm down,* I screamed in my head. *You're going to pull the wiring loose and electrocute me.* All my fear of shock from the electric lines came back to me and I had a moment where I came pretty close to panic. I started to fight the powerful tugs, trying to turn away and pull the line loose— and that's when I saw the first one. It froze me in place. And as I hung there in the water, the first was followed by a dozen more.

I said I thought they were needlefish. They weren't. As the first one swam into view in the circle of light I could tell what they were, and even underwater I could feel the hair stand up on my neck. Far worse than sharks, or moray eels, or anything else I could think of—this was the worst luck imaginable.

Swarming into the area I had to cross to get to the boat—schooling around the boat itself—were dozens, even hundreds, of sea snakes. The water was alive with them. All of them swimming into the beam of my floodlight—and I was being pulled up into the deadly swarm. At the time, I didn't know much about the species—but I didn't need to. Because I knew that sea snakes are the most venomous of all serpents.

That's right. The most venomous serpent on earth, deadlier than the king cobra, the black mamba—the venom from one bite of one of these reptiles could kill a full-grown bull elephant in under five seconds. And there were now more than a hundred of them in the water around me.

My mind filled with images of my wife and sons back in Key West. My life shouldn't end here, not this way. I wasn't ready. I wanted to live. But at the moment I didn't see how to do that trick. Still, I knew what I couldn't do—I couldn't go up where the snakes were. So I kicked with all my might and tried to go back down toward the sea floor.

And the snakes followed.

I didn't know what to think or what to do. I dodged, twisted, turned as much as the lifeline would let me, and the snakes followed. I had never heard that they were this aggressive. Why were they chasing me? Could I be between them and their nest? I swam left—they followed. I dodged right—so did they. And they were getting closer all the time, swarming straight at me like moths to a flame.

Well, maybe you guessed it already. When the nickel dropped for me, I was filled with an incredible sense of relief. *It wasn't me they were chasing—it was the light!*

I was so happy I yelled—and got a mouthful of water for my trouble. I kicked backward, watching the snakes chase closer as I fumbled with the light. The whole pack of them was coming at me in a kind of chain-mail pattern that would have been pretty if it wasn't so damned deadly. The leaders of this snake-chain were less than six feet from me when I finally got the floodlight off my belt. I flung it as far from me as I could. The light rushed quickly away from me, pulled straight up by the tugging on the wire, and the wiggling train of snakes bent up and followed the light toward the surface.

I relaxed a little. The worst was over. I could just bide my time on the bottom now, until the snakes went away or swam to the stern where the spotlight was shining. And then I could climb out at the opposite end of the boat, and that would be that.

Or so I thought. But as I tried to settle down and take a deep breath, I found it impossible. There was nothing coming through the hose, no air at all. *They've cut off my air,* I thought. And I knew I couldn't stay down until the snakes went away. I had to swim right straight through the slithering bastards, or stay here and drown.

It was no choice at all. Either way I'd be dead—and if I

tried to get through the snakes and didn't make it, well, at least I'd tried.

I let out a breath and followed my own air bubbles to the surface. The *Pilar*'s hull appeared like the sun eclipsed by the moon. The surface around the stern was living waves of sea snakes. Like hundreds of moths drawn to the light, the snakes swarmed around *Pilar*'s stern.

To my very great relief, there didn't seem to be any of the wriggling bastards at the bow. So that's where I headed—far from the light and the snakes.

I surfaced at the darkest spot of water I could find, just off the port side of the bow. I took a moment just to gulp down air. Amazing how good it tastes, just plain air, when you've been without for a while. I swam out along the port side to better see and hear what the crew was experiencing in the cockpit.

Fuentes and Winston were wrapping up the cables from my air and floodlight, the two Cubans were smacking the side of the *Pilar* with the persuader and a bait knife, and Papa stood at the stern firing the tommy gun in short bursts at the pooling snakes.

The persuader was Papa's sawed-off baseball bat, used to knock out big-game fish. Julius had natural rhythm and was using the club almost like a drumstick. But with his adrenaline pumping, he was denting the side of the *Pilar.*

Papa's voice rose over the others. "Watch the goddamned

wood. Watch it, I say!" He rattled off another round at the snakes, *ploit, ploit, ploit, ploit, ploit, ploit, ploit.*

Patche yelled to Julius, "*¡Mira, mira, míralos!*" Look, look, look at them! The big man leaned over and whacked two snakes pushing their way through the transom's through-hull fittings.

Papa let loose another round, *ploit, ploit, ploit, ploit, ploit, ploit, ploit.*

"Get that one, it's coming up the hose," Winston yelled. Patche sliced the head off a colorful two-footer.

Julius turned and saw three more wriggling in over the side. He clubbed them on the deck and cursed the little bastards in Spanish.

Papa fired another round into the water just off the stern.

"Good God, when will it end?" Winston demanded.

"Baron?!" Papa yelled into the dark. "Where the hell are you?" He pulled back on the trigger and sprayed the surface in frustration. *Ploit, ploit, ploit, ploit, ploit, ploit, ploit.* His line of fire raced across the surface and passed me by only a few feet.

I ducked away and answered, "Over here," and kicked toward the boat. It then hit me that they hadn't realized the snakes were attracted to the lights. "Kill the lights," I screamed.

They must have heard me because Papa turned and fired on the floodlight over the cockpit. Then in the dark I heard him say, "Put a weight on that thing and toss it over." A second later there was a splash, and the glow from my light, still on its cable, fluttered back and forth as it sank to the bottom.

"Look at them go," Winston said. "They're following it straight to Davy Jones."

I waited a few minutes longer to make sure I didn't swim into any stragglers. Papa gave me a hand climbing back on board. "Are you okay?"

"Yes. I think I'll live," I answered him as I caught sight of one of the dead snakes on the deck. Its body glistened in the moonlight. You could make out the yellowish-green hue flecked with black, and the heavy black circles around the body. Though it was only a few feet long, the body was as thick around as my arm. I was surprised by how much it still looked like a land snake. Only its flattened tail gave away its watery origins.

"A miracle, lad," Winston said, patting my shoulder. "If just one of those nasty vipers had his way, we would have been giving you last rites."

"Sorry to disappoint," I laughed. "I've still got the old Hemingstein luck."

"I'm glad to have you among the breathing," Papa said, grinning. "Now, enough kidding around. Did you find where the Krauts ran aground?"

"Yeah, about seventy-five feet off your starboard." I pulled off my wet shirt and grabbed a towel. "She was headed north-by-northwest."

"Great work, Baron. Gentlemen, we're going sub hunting tonight."

"What do you want to do about the light?" Patche asked in Spanish.

Papa held down the kill switch on the generator and it coughed a few times before falling silent. In the water below us the light winked out. "Bring her up. The flame's out. The slimy bastards will have no interest now."

Papa went below to the *Pilar*'s cabin while the rest of the crew pulled anchor, started the engines, and stowed gear. When Ernesto came back up he had with him two bottles of gin and several glasses. "A toast to a successful mission, friends." We took our drinks. "If our luck holds," he continued, "we'll find them headed back to Berlin with a bent prop or worse."

"By the amount of damage to the reef, I'm surprised they're still floating."

"What was it like down there?" Papa asked.

"Beautiful," I said, remembering the way the colors had leapt at me out of the dark. "But scary, too, and all the feelings in between. The sea snakes must have had their nest where the sub hit. They were like bees without a hive."

"Damn glad you didn't get bit."

"Me too."

Fuentes brought the *Pilar* past the breakwater and took the heading north-by-northwest. We were moving at a solid ten knots with the Gulf Stream pushing us another five.

I looked back at the white water rolling over the reef. "You know, in a few more years an island will be born there."

"We'll call it Cayo Ernesto," Julius joked.

"No, no," Papa answered, laughing. "The Baron found it. It's his island."

SEVENTEEN

PROFESSOR," my mother interrupted, "you do know that Les really did build an island, don't you?"

"Really! Cayo Ernesto?"

"Hell, no," Dad answered. "That kind of crap would have turned Papa's stomach. Besides, there's only one name fit to give an island raised from the sea."

"And what's that?" the professor asked.

"New Atlantis, of course," Dad said, and Charlie started humming "My Country 'Tis of Thee" in the background.

"You actually built an island in the ocean?" the professor asked.

"Not just an island," Willeford interrupted, for a moment dropping his slightly off-key humming. "You're looking at the president of his own country."

"President? Is that legal?"

"It sure is—everything by the book," Daddy said, and now Charlie swung into "Hail to the Chief." My mother said, "Charlie, please, pick a key. Any key at all."

Daddy ignored the bantering and went on. "We raised New Atlantis on a sea mount, about six miles off Jamaica's coast. We declared our sovereignty on July 4, 1964."

"Why there?"

"The ocean depth surrounding the sea mount is about one thousand feet, but at the mount we were twenty-five feet from the surface, and this is most important—we were in international waters. Do you know why that's important, Professor?"

"Not actually, no."

"When most of us get good and fed up with civilization, we dream of escaping to a tropical island. Am I right?"

"Yes, of course. But—"

"But there aren't any. Not any more. In this day and age, even the most remote spit of land is claimed by one government or another. But if an island was to rise up in international waters it could be claimed as a sovereign country."

"Are you sure this isn't *The Mouse That Roared*?" the professor suggested.

"Bingo," my mother cheered.

"A fine book"—Daddy laughed—"and not too far from the awful truth. Think about it, 1964. A few years earlier the United States was dealing with the Cuban missile crisis. You can see why New Atlantis gained the attention of the U.S. State Department. Of course, their interest was to see if we were large enough to provide a possible southern listening-post."

"You mean you were trying to get the CIA to bankroll the building of the island?"

"That would have been grand," Mom said, laughing. "Unfortunately, we sank our own money into this dream."

"It was a gamble, and if it had paid off, it would have paid out big. The idea was to build an artificial reef on a sea mount that could support a sand bank. It wasn't going to be big—say a hundred yards wide and half a mile long. Ultimately, we planned for a small hotel, a post office, and a lighthouse with a shortwave transmitter.

"A post office? Why not a casino?" the professor said with oily innocence.

"I meant it to be honorable. I thought about a marine lab, like Mike Learner had in Bimini."

"But how would you make money?"

"That's the beauty part. You start with stamps—every country has stamps. New Atlantis's first issue honored President Johnson. After that we featured Winston Churchill, Hubert Humphrey, and our returning POWs."

"Tell him about the scruples, Les." Willeford laughed. "I just love this."

"What?" asked the professor.

"Scruples, man, you must know what they are," Dad said. "Even you must have a few. In New Atlantis, that was the name of our official currency. Because like dollars, a man can never have enough scruples. Our exchange rate was roughly equal to Uncle Sam's. But the real trick was to get recognized by the World Trade Organization. Then it's as simple as printing your own money."

"This is incredible. Why have I never heard about this? What happened?"

"The hurricane seasons of 'sixty-four and 'sixty-five," Mom answered.

JEFF STOPPED THE TAPE. "Wow—I always wondered how your dad came up with the idea for New Atlantis. I'll never forget the first time I heard him tell my folks about it. I was twelve—we were at that funny round house down in the Keys—and I thought, 'What a great idea!'"

"Yeah," I said. "It was a great idea, but—"

"My grandpa was a president?" Bear interrupted. "A real president?"

"Yes, indeed. He took his dream and made it real. At least for a few years." I smiled. "I remembered for years after he would still greet friends with a warm 'Ho, Nobles,' or, if it was a woman, 'Your Ladyship.' He gave everyone a title. I have a paper somewhere that states that I am a Lady of the Republic of New Atlantis."

"I bet it's in one of the boxes," Jeff said. "I found one full of New Atlantis photos and stamps."

"I want to see, I want to see," Bear shouted.

"Okay," Jeff said, "hold your horses." He disappeared down the hall for a minute and I heard the closet door open and close.

"This is fun, isn't it, Mom?" Bear grinned.

"Yeah," I laughed. "I'm kinda glad you're getting to know your grandpa."

"Check it out," Jeff said as he spread the contents of a box across the bed.

"Wow, this is cool," Bear said, picking up the stamp sheets. Jeff picked up one of a dozen newspaper clippings. I looked at the photos of the island.

"Can we use these stamps on our Christmas cards?" Bear asked.

"No, honey, these are collector's items," Jeff told her. He held out a clipping from *The New York Times.* "Look at this.

Your dad creates his own country and the headline is still about Hemingway's little brother. Talk about living in a shadow."

I forced a smile. "Once after I won a powerboat race, the headline was 'Young Woman and the Sea,' and Dad said, 'Hillsides, don't worry about it. If you had been the first woman on the moon, they'd still sell papers with a picture of Papa. The important thing in life is to discover who you are—not who you're related to.' "

I flipped to the next picture. It showed my father standing on a raised bamboo platform on the island. His hands were held up in a mighty cheer, while his eyes squinted out at the Caribbean sun.

"Look at that grin." I tapped the photo. "After all these years, I had forgotten. Your grandpa and I had some pretty good adventures of our own."

"Like him and his brother?"

"No sea snakes or dragons, but once we faced a monster storm in a little boat."

Jeffry smiled and touched my hand. "That's what you were thinking about earlier, when you stopped the tape," he said.

"Yes," I said. "That's it."

"Have I heard this one?" he asked me.

"You say you've heard them all—twice."

"That's right, I have," he said, pretending not to look at Bear. "Never mind." And he reached for the Play button.

"No, wait, tell me, tell me," Bear said frantically.

"Oh, you don't want to hear this," Jeff teased her.

"I do! I really do!"

"Well—"

"Mom, please?"

I smiled. "I was older than you—thirteen—and my dad had been asked to bring a sailboat back to Miami from Bimini. The owner was afraid to make the trip because the motor didn't work. Now this shouldn't have been a problem. Just sail due west for eight hours and you're bound to hit Florida somewhere. And Daddy hated engines anyway. He'd made the trip plenty of times with just sail. Nothing to it. It was so easy that Dad ordered me to buy only one gallon of water and one loaf of bread. Like I said, this was supposed to be a quick trip."

"A three-hour cruise," Jeff sang.

"Right. And as we sailed out of Bimini Harbor, Dad said, 'Hillsides, we're going to have a *great* adventure.' Now let me tell you, 'great' was an interesting word to my father. He used it a lot. 'We're going to have a *great* day, a *great* adventure, it was *great* seeing you.' Only, 'great' never meant easy or simple. It meant exciting, painful, pleasing, and most of all memorable.

"And that's what this trip was. We left about an hour before sunset. Dad did his best to avoid sun. Now, before this trip I'd never had a problem sailing at night with Dad, but then, I had never encountered the Devil's Triangle's freakish weather before, either."

"Do you know what the Devil's Triangle is, Bear?" Jeff asked her.

"Nope."

"Well, it's an area between Florida and the Bahamas where a lot of ships and planes have gone down. They just disappear, and nobody knows why. But I don't believe the Devil has anything to do with it. It's just a place where a lot of storms come up hard and fast."

"And you were stuck in there, Mommy?" she asked.

"Not stuck, honey," I told her. "But we were in it. When we had wind, it was gale-force, with gusts over fifty knots. So we'd take our sails down and batten down the hatches. But after the storm passed there was nothing, absolutely dead calm. Not a breath of air. This happened several times the first night. The next day, we found the same thing. Big storms followed by flat calms. Finally, after twenty hours at sea, Dad suggested we leave the sail up and try to run with the next squall breeze."

"Eek," said Jeff, and again, "If not for the courage of its fearless crew, the *Minnow* would be lost."

"That's about the size of it," I said. "The storm hit and the seas built to over twelve feet. We had a lot of water crashing on deck. It was kinda cool at first. We looked like the cover of *Sail* magazine, knifing our way through these big waves.

"Then we saw it. This nasty gray cloud shaped like an ice cream cone slowly forming and dropping down toward the ocean's surface. 'Hillsides, that's a waterspout,' my dad yelled, 'Better get the canvas down quick.'

"I had never seen a waterspout before. I didn't even know it was dangerous, until I saw it was spinning like a tornado. But what could a tornado do at sea? I thought. Pick up a fish and fling it?

"I made my way back to the mast, keeping my eye on the spinning gray cone. The waves were beginning to whip up a white froth. I knew this storm was different, but I had no idea of the danger we were in. After all, I was with my daddy. And he didn't seem too worried—in fact, he was laughing. So why should I be worried?"

"Um—common sense?" Jeff suggested.

I laughed. "Not a long suit in my family," I answered.

"Daddy, don't interrupt," Bear said. "What happened, Mommy? What about the tornado?"

"The waterspout continued to drop closer to the surface," I said. "And as it did the wind got stronger. And stronger.

"It was just like you hear in the movies," I told Bear. "The wind sounded like a freight train going by overhead, and then it would rise up to shriek like some kind of awful ghost. I looked at my dad, steering the boat into this storm, and I said, 'Daddy, are we going to be all right?' He smiled and said, 'Don't sweat it, kid. Take care of that sail.'

"I found that I couldn't wrap up the sails. There was too

much wind pulling against them, so Dad yelled, 'Better tie them down quick. We've only a few minutes now.' And he yelled out, 'Isn't this *great*?'

"I was beginning to wonder about that, but I bumped and crawled my way to the bow where I used the anchor line to wrap around the jib. The sail gave off a steady *thump, thump, thump,* like a deafening heartbeat. But slowly I got the ropes to squeeze the air from the sail.

"Now all this time my attention had been on the sail. I hadn't looked at the waterspout in several minutes. So imagine my surprise when I turned and found this swirling monstrosity just a half-mile off our starboard bow. It was whirling ferociously, a greenish-blackish furious thing, and the water near it was all whipped up into flying foam. And that's when it finally hit me that this thing was *dangerous.* I don't even think I could breathe, I was so scared.

"I looked up at this thousand-foot-long gray-black giant, twisting violently like the Mad Hatter's drill, and I felt my stomach drop. I watched hopelessly as it sucked up thousands of tons of water and sprayed them out again in a wide circle. There was no way we were going to outrun it.

"The rain picked up as the monster closed in. I covered my face and held on to the deck. The drops were now hitting so hard they felt like bees stinging. The roar of the wind had our mainsail shrouds howling. And we were heeled so far over, each counter-wave seemed to wash right into the cockpit. I was sure we were going to sink.

"There was no hope of getting the mainsail down, it was all I could do just to hold on. I looked back at Dad holding the tiller. He was soaked to the bone, but his face didn't show fear. Instead he was angry, like a kid who wanted to leave the park with the game ball. Nature wasn't playing by the rules and he wanted out.

"But there wasn't any 'out' to go to. The ocean all around us was roaring and screaming like a wounded wild animal. Then I felt a terrific pressure on my face and my chest, and the air burst from my lungs. I couldn't breathe. Our little boat rose from the water like some child's toy, and was tossed to the side. And then came the sickening fall. The splash was huge. The waves rose up as tall as the mast. I didn't know they could come that big. Then the waves crashed on deck and it felt like a water-flume ride gone bad. My eyes were stinging from the salt, my heart was racing, and my stomach was somewhere at the top of my throat, ready to hurl out of my mouth and into the water.

"Then I spotted the funnel. It was moving off, away from us, like a drunk driver, swerving from side to side. We were safe. Or that's what I thought. That's when I heard my father yell, *'Duck!'*

"I looked up to see our wooden mast crack like a broken

pencil. It's strange now, thinking about it, but it sounded just like a tree falling in a forest. I tried to dive out of the way, but I slipped on a tangle of lines. And before I could even call out, I was over the side and under the water."

"Mom!" Bear said, clearly terrified.

"It's okay," Jeff told her. "There's a happy ending." It was what he had always told her when he read her bedtime stories that set off her overactive imagination.

"Is there, Mom?" Bear asked.

"I'm here," I said.

"But how?"

"Well—I came up about twenty feet behind the boat. Before I could panic, I felt the steady tug of my tether harness. The line had held—I was still attached to the boat."

"Whew," said Bear.

"But I was being dragged through the water and in and out of rising waves. I should have been okay with that. It wasn't like I was drowning. But I couldn't shake my fear. See, just the week before I had seen a movie called *Jaws*. It really ruined swimming in the ocean for me. I was now more scared of being attacked by sharks than I was of that waterspout."

"Wow, what did you do?" Bear asked.

"I began pulling myself toward the boat, hand over hand along the lifeline. Every time I tried to take a breath, I got half air and half water. By the time I reached the boat, I was exhausted. It's funny, it was that movie and my fear of sharks that saved me."

I looked back at my daughter. "When I finally did get close enough to the boat, your grandpa grabbed my arm. Now you know he wouldn't hurt me on purpose, but when he pulled me up out of the water, he pulled so hard it dislocated my shoulder."

"Is that like broken?" Bear asked.

"It means pulled out of the socket," Jeff told her.

"Ooowww," Bear said. "That's gotta hurt."

"Yeah, well, let's just say the first words out of my mouth were not 'Thank you.' But Dad did push it back into place quickly, and after a few hours the pain wasn't so bad."

"Wait a minute, hold on." Bear stopped me and began to laugh. "Grandma told me you dislocated your shoulder climbing trees. Are you making this up?"

"Ha—she's got you!" Jeff laughed.

"Could I make up this much detail? I'm not a storyteller, like Dad."

"Oh, certainly not," Jeff said.

"I fell out of the tree when I was seven and out of a boat at thirteen."

"I don't know," Jeff said with a wink at Bear. "Your whole family seems to enjoy embellishing their accomplishments."

"What's that mean?" Bear asked.

"It means that your mom is part of a tribe that loves to tell a good story. Even if it means making it up," Jeff answered.

"Don't you think this explains my fear of sailing at night? And you know how I hate the sound of high wind."

"It doesn't matter if we believe you," Jeff said. "It's still a good story."

"Dad's right. But I want to know how you got home," Bear said.

"Wait, I got it," Jeff said. "Towed home by a Nazi U-boat out of a time warp! Or wait—a UFO!"

"Not quite," I laughed. "But very close."

"Really?" said Bear.

"Yup. On the second night out—I guess it was about ten o'clock, the whole sky suddenly lit up. It was like night turned to day."

"What was it?" Bear demanded.

"Imagine the brightest light you can, shining down on you. It's so bright, you can't see anything but what's in the light."

"Cool, it really was a UFO?" Bear asked.

"Nope. When I stepped out of the cabin, I heard the huge diesels approaching. Dad yelled, 'Must be a Coast Guard cutter.' I was never so happy in my life to hear those words. Keep in mind I had just spent the last eight hours bailing water from our cabin with a bucket.

"It took a few minutes for the light to come closer. It was

so bright we shielded our eyes with our hands. Dad ordered me up front to throw the tow line."

"What about your shoulder?" Bear asked, and Jeff said, "Good for you, Bear."

I smiled at them both. "Of course I used my good arm. I held the bow line like this," I said, and coiled the curtain cord. I leaned back, swinging my arm. "I waited until they were within a couple of yards. And just when I thought, 'Okay, now they're close enough,' the ship killed the spotlight. That's when Dad and I saw that four hundred feet of oceangoing freighter had just passed in front of us at full speed.

"Truthfully, I was glad for the blinding light. Because without it we would have seen this big ship barreling down at us and died from fright."

"Well, if they didn't save you, who did?" my daughter asked.

"Remember Grandpa talking about Life Lesson 101? 'Never believe in anyone more than in yourself'? Well, the next morning Dad and I took inventory of what we had. A dead battery, no radio, a cup of fresh water, two slices of bread, a broken motor, and a snapped mast.

"I still remember Dad smiling as he said, 'All is not lost, not by any means, daughter. We can still sail using the Bimini top. And at the next rain, just put out a couple of pans and cups. Nothing is quite as sweet as God's juice.'

"See, my dad was still having fun. I don't know if he loved

the danger, or just loved tempting Mother Nature. But it was times like this that he seemed most alive, most in control."

"So finish the story," Bear demanded. "How did you get home?"

"A storm did come up. It was ugly, but nothing compared to surviving a waterspout.

"When the heavy rains and winds hit, we lowered the Bimini top to an angle that made a perfect downwind, square-rig sail. We were pushed due west. Right where we needed to go. I remember the happy grin Dad had holding the tiller. He said, 'Hillsides—now this is living!'

"A couple of hours later we finally sighted land. A large fishing boat came up and Dad talked the captain into giving us a tow. We put in just above Palm Beach."

"That's some trip," Jeff said.

"Yeah, it sure was," I said, and for a few moments I was back there again with Daddy. The sound of the waves against the hull, the many creaks and clicks and ripples of a boat under sail; the reassuring sight of Daddy with the tiller in his hand and a quiet grin on his face.

I looked up to see Bear and Jeffry looking at me.

"Earth to Mom," Bear said.

"I was just remembering," I said.

Jeffry leaned forward and brushed my cheek. He held his hand out, showing me a tear glittering on his fingertip. "It sounded like a good memory," he said.

"It was," I told him, wiping at my cheek. "But I was realizing something, too. The greatest gift my father gave me was the lesson that *life* is the adventure. No matter what it dishes out—you can make it. That's why—well . . ." my voice trailed off.

"What?" Bear asked.

"Why it's hard to accept—how—" My voice broke and I wiped another tear. "It's hard for me to accept the way Daddy died." I was crying a little now. Jeff put a hand on my back.

"I miss my father," I said, letting out a breath. "I really miss who he was—before he got sick." I fought for control, looking at Bear. She looked so worried. Most kids don't know how to handle it when Mommy cries, and she was more sensitive than a lot of children. I hated to cry in front of her, but I felt so damned small. More child than mother. I suddenly felt as if I had just lost both parents. "This damned tape," I said.

"Mommy, tell me—how did Grandpa die?" Bear asked.

"Not now, sweetie," Jeff said quickly, but I held up a hand.

"It's okay," I said. "She needs to know, and now is as good a time as any."

"Know what?" Bear said. "What's wrong with dying? Doesn't everybody do it?"

"Yeah," I said. "Everybody does." I wiped my face and took a breath. Bear was a sensitive, caring girl—which made her question that much harder.

At what age is a child ready to hear about suicide? How

could I explain her grandfather's death without ruining her image of a courageous, adventuresome man? On the one hand, he was the man who taught me how to be brave and love life. But he was also a man who had taken his own life. I could not make both those ideas fit the same man. His ending almost made the rest seem like a lie—but it wasn't, I was sure it wasn't. How could I explain that to my daughter when I couldn't even make sense of it for myself?

Bear was looking up at me, waiting. I was hoping that if I could put this into words that made sense for my daughter, maybe I could finally understand, too. "Your grandpa," I began, "felt—that his body had betrayed him."

"What?" she asked. "What does that mean?"

My mind rushed with images: doctors' offices, hospital rooms, waiting rooms. Daddy at the doctor's, Daddy waving good-bye with his hands clasped above his head, Daddy on the floor with the gun beside him. I closed my eyes and heard Jeff explain while the pictures flooded my memory.

"It means your grandpa's body turned against him," Jeff was saying.

"But—we *are* our body," Bear said.

"We're either a lot more, or we're nothing," Jeff told her. "Grandpa thought his body was slowly dying, and killing the things that made him who he was."

"I still don't get how your body can kill you," Bear said.

And I could tell that she was upset. But we were too far in to back off now.

"Diabetes," I answered, opening my eyes. "He was sick with diabetes."

It was simple and true. *She'll accept that,* I thought. And diabetes had killed him. Forget the know-it-all doctors who say that nobody actually dies from diabetes. Of course they don't; they die from heart failure, liver failure, loss of circulation, depression, and, of course, suicide. But nobody dies from the disease itself. Nobody lives that long.

"Diabetes, really?" Bear asked, sensing there was more that I was not saying.

"Well, in a manner of speaking. Look—the kind of diabetes that runs in the Hemingway family doesn't happen until you're much, much older. So don't worry."

"Okay, but how does it work?"

"It, um, destroys your body from the inside out—to your grandfather it made death look a whole lot better than life."

"But Grandpa wasn't afraid," Bear said, looking between Jeff and me. "Was he?" There was a trace of uncertainty in her smile.

"He wasn't afraid," Jeff told her. "Not of anything."

"Then—I don't get it," Bear said. I could tell she was trying to figure out if one should fear death. I tried to reassure her.

"Honey, your grandpa loved adventure. He loved to test

himself and he had absolute confidence in his abilities. Diabetes took that from him. It rots you from the inside out."

I paused, because this was actually making sense to me. For the first time in fifteen years I was not thinking of *how* my father had died, but *why* he chose to end his life. "You want to know my first clue that your grandpa was sick? It was a hot, muggy June day and he came into the room and said, 'Hillsides, I'm covered in sweat, but my feet are ice-cold. What do you think it is?' Well, I didn't know and he didn't know."

"It doesn't sound so bad," Bear said.

"It kind of was," I said, "because his feet being cold was just the first symptom. Dad went over to Bimini the next weekend, the usual newspaper business. Something happened and he stubbed his big toe. Considering everything he'd been through, no big deal. But his toe never healed. By the time he saw a doctor, they had to schedule surgery to restore blood-flow. His feet were cold because diabetes had collapsed his veins."

"Yuck. What did they do to fix him?"

"His doctors changed his diet: no alcohol, no sugar, no salt. Dad lost about fifty pounds in the first month. But as a diabetic he still craved sugar." How well I remembered that craving. The times Daddy tried to sneak sweets, as if he could fool his body and the disease as easily as he fooled us. It had been almost funny at times—almost. "Once we heard the car horn blowing in the driveway. Your grandma ran out and found

Grandpa bent over the steering wheel. She was sure he'd suffered a heart attack, but then he sat up."

"What was it?" Jeff asked.

"He was sneaking a quart of ice cream and an apple pie before dinner."

"Wow." Bear laughed. "So, Grandpa knew sugar was bad, but he still ate it? Because he loved life?" To Bear, ice cream and pie were the stuff of life itself, and to risk being sick to eat them—that was raw courage and real adventure. But I shook my head. We had started this, and I needed her to understand.

"No, honey. That's not it. This wasn't one of Grandpa's adventures. This was the disease making him do things he knew he shouldn't do. Unless you live with a diabetic," I told her, "you won't understand. Their bodies crave the sugar, even though they can't process it. And the mood swings, wow."

"I don't get that," Bear said.

"One minute you're happier than you've ever been in your life and filled with energy. The next second—boom. You just want to lie down—you feel like you hate the world and everybody in it."

"Like you and Daddy when you have a book deadline?"

"Something like that," I answered, laughing. "But with my family, it's a permanent deadline."

"Let's just say the Hemingways are famous for their mood swings," Jeff said. "Not your mother, of course," he added quickly, ducking an imaginary punch.

"Look, today we know the swings are brought on by our blood-sugar level. Give us sugar and we're up. Without it we crash and get grumpy."

"*Really* grumpy," Jeff added.

"You mean sad?" Bear asked.

"It's more than just being sad. A diabetic depression makes you blow up at small things. Sometimes—well, you have a hard time focusing. Begin one project, then change to another. Meanwhile, your organs are constantly threatening to close down. Living with a diabetic, having diabetes—it's a daily challenge."

"Do you have the disease?" Bear asked me with an anxious look on her face.

"No, but it runs in our family. My brother Peter and your Aunt Annie have it, and so did our father, Uncle Ernest, and Grandfather Hemingway. It probably goes back further, but they only started testing for it in the last seventy years. And there's only been real treatment in the last ten. So when Uncle Ernest was at the Mayo Clinic—they didn't treat his diabetes, they treated his depression."

"How?" Bear asked.

"Shock treatments. They hook up your brain and kind of cook it with electricity."

"Gross." Bear made a face.

"Yeah. Hard to believe they thought it helped. But for some people, it does. They forget all about why they were depressed. In fact, they forget everything for a while. Now, can you think why this would be a really bad treatment for a writer?"

"If you can't remember, what do you write about?"

"Bingo," Jeff said. "You're robbing them. You're stealing the very memories they need to create stories. Which of course makes them even more depressed when they can't write any more."

"And that's why Grandpa *and* Uncle Ernest died?"

"That's right."

"Oh. Okay," Bear said. She frowned and sat quietly for a minute. We all did. Then she looked up again.

"So okay, wait a second," Bear said. "I'm confused." She glanced between us. "They died from diabetes, or electricity?"

"Neither one," I said and I had to pause before I finally came out with the sentence I had been avoiding. "They died because they shot themselves."

EIGHTEEN

WHAT?" Bear was stunned. "You mean with a *gun*?" This was the first she had heard of her grandpa's suicide. I didn't want to ruin her budding friendship with her grandfather, but now I had to explain it.

"Having diabetes gives you very real and logical reasons to be depressed. At the end of your grandpa's life, he faced amputation of both legs and loss of his eyesight. Your great-uncle Ernest's weight dropped from two hundred ten pounds when he was healthy to a sickly one fifty-five. Do you understand—they became shells of who they used to be."

"So they were afraid of dying," Bear said.

"No," I told her. "I don't believe they were afraid of death. They were afraid of continuing a diminished life."

"What's diminished mean?"

"Less than it was. Less than it should be," Jeff said.

"Like Grandma?" Bear asked.

"Exactly," I swallowed hard. I hadn't made the connection. Mom's lung cancer had taken her through long courses of radiation and chemotherapy treatments. She had been bridled with an oxygen tube and confined to a medical bed, yet she fought on. And when doctors gave her six months, she lived another six years. Perhaps that was the difference in how I thought of my parents' deaths. Mom fought for life and by the time death took her, *I* was ready.

"Do you remember what I said when Grandma died?"

"You said—she's in heaven."

"Yes," I looked at Jeff. "I also said, when she died it was the most beautiful moment in my life, next to your birth."

"But you loved Grandma?" Bear questioned.

"I still do. I loved her so much, I didn't want to see her suffer anymore. When she died, your Aunt Annie and I were beside her, holding her hands. We told her we loved her. We told her it was okay to let go. The hospice minister said a prayer and that's when the angels came for her."

"Mom. Angels?"

"Yes. I really believe that. Your grandma turned her head

from us and looked at the door and smiled, like somebody had just come into the room. Somebody she loved a lot and hadn't seen for a while. There were three of them, and she greeted each one with a smile and her eyes followed them as they moved to her bedside."

"What did she say?"

"She didn't say anything. But it was clear that she was seeing something. She was so happy. Then when the last one came in, a tear rolled down from her eye and she let out the most beautiful laugh and I knew. It was your grandfather. Only my daddy could make Mom laugh like that. And your Aunt Annie and I cried. We knew Mom was going off to a great party." I wiped at my tears with my sleeve and looked up to see Bear staring at me with a solemn, questioning expression. I took her hand.

"Grandma gave me a great gift, too. I wanted to believe in life after death, but I didn't. Not after my father died. The night after that happened, I sat up all night on the tile floor where he had died and I waited. I waited all night long. I wanted some kind of sign. Something—anything. Something that said goodbye. I sat there all night, but there was nothing. He hadn't left us any note, or any sign that—" I stopped for a moment and let the tears come. "Oh, hell," I finally said. "I wanted to see his ghost. I wanted him to return from the grave to say he was sorry and he missed me. And he didn't. Nothing. So when

Grandma passed, I felt like I had finally had a chance to say good-bye to both of them."

I ran out of things to say and just looked at Bear. She looked away, clearly thinking it all over. She would either believe it or not. It was up to her. Finally she looked up at me and gave me a dazzling smile.

"I think this tape is good," Bear said.

"Why?" I asked.

"Because you talk about Grandpa with a smile, instead of tears."

Jeff whispered, "How'd you get so smart?" and I gave my daughter a hug.

"Just lucky." Bear grinned.

"Does anybody feel up to hearing the end of the tape?" Jeff asked. "We're pretty close now."

"Absolutely," I agreed, and pushed the Play button on the Barney tape machine.

"A hurricane?" the professor asked. "But don't you have them every year?"

"They don't have 'em in Wisconsin," Mom said drily.

"That was the worst season I can remember," my father said. "The storms came screaming across the ocean at us, one after another. There was no way we could have predicted that.

And no way our little country could survive it, either." Dad paused, and the fire crackled in the background. "And so New Atlantis, like her namesake, slipped back into the sea. We couldn't afford to rebuild."

"It should still be a book," Mom countered.

"Speaking of shoulds—we've got to wrap this up. I have to be at Junior's at first light."

"Junior's—what's that?" the professor asked.

"It's the best place in Miami to hitch a ride to Bimini."

"Bimini? The island where Ernest and Mike Learner set world records in billfish?"

"Oh, give it a rest," Willeford replied, laughing. "Les is the editor of the *Bimini Out-Island News.* Les, I can't thank you enough. It's been truly fun. Doris, thank you again."

"Our pleasure, Charles," Mom answered.

"You're a good sport, Herr Doktor Professor." I heard a thumping that must have been Daddy giving one of his famous poundings to the professor's back. "Charles, take care of this man. He needs help. Oh, for Christ's sake, turn that thing off."

THE TAPE THUMPED into silence and then snapped back on with the heavy hum of diesel boat motors. The professor's voice rose over the sound of the engines. "Tell me, Les, why did you choose to run a newspaper in Bimini?"

"A boat!" Bear said. "They're on a boat, Mom! You can hear it!"

Indeed you could. The sound of the wind moving across the microphone was clear, and faintly, behind the steady throb of the engines, you could hear water splashing and slapping against the hull.

Jeffry stopped the tape, laughing. "I don't believe it!" he said. "This guy has brass—um, guts," he amended, looking at Bear. "He's hitched a ride to Bimini with your dad! He's a real Hemingleech, all right."

"What's a Hemingleech?" Bear said.

I had to smile, too. "It's what your dad calls people like this professor. They all want to own a little piece of your great-uncle Ernest."

"So?" she said. "Why don't they just read his books?"

"Out of the mouths of babes," Jeff said.

"That's not enough for some people. They need more. They turn Ernest into a kind of religion. They want to be like him, do what he did—"

"Sometimes without all the mess and bother of reading all those long hard books," Jeff said.

"I don't get it," Bear said.

I patted her hand. "Sometimes I don't, either," I said.

"But isn't it okay to like Uncle Ernest?"

"Of course it is," I said. "It's just that some people take it too far."

"Like what?"

"We met a guy in Italy," Jeff told her. "He didn't even say hello. Just walked up to your mom and started pulling out papers proving that he was Ernest's son, and waving around a big book he'd written that showed how to redesign the universe based on Ernest Hemingway."

"He was crazy," Bear said.

Jeff laughed again. "Uh-uh. He was a respected college professor."

"Just like the guy in Grandpa's story!"

"Now you're getting it," I said.

"Is this guy going to do something like that?" she asked.

I laughed. I was starting to feel a lot better. "Let's find out," I said, and pushed Play.

"—the people are great. And the water," Daddy was saying. "There's no prettier place than Bimini anywhere on earth."

"Of course, part of the charm must be that Ernest wrote so well about—"

"Oh, for crying out loud. I've been going to Bimini for the last forty years. I know every man, woman, and child there. I've written up their birth announcements and their obits. Christ on a bun, man."

"I'm sorry, I didn't mean—well—to get off on the wrong foot again."

"You've got a talent for it," Dad snorted. "So far I haven't seen that you even have a right foot."

"I am sorry. I didn't get much sleep. I'm not really thinking clearly. But, uh—some of those stories you told last night—"

"What about 'em?"

"Well, just, ah—wonderfully told, you know."

"Spit out the butter, Professor."

"Well, it's just that—Willeford said some of the stories might not be completely true."

"Charlie said that?"

"Well—yes."

"You believe him?"

"I don't know. I'm not sure what I believe."

"Well, there's your problem."

"Yes, but—I mean, I would like to know the truth, you know."

"Truth is a strange thing, kid," Dad answered.

"Ho, Les," a new voice called out over the roar of engines. "You and the doc want to come up to the bridge?"

"Happily, Captain," Dad yelled. Then, conversationally, "Watch your head, or we'll be mopping up gray matter." The tape thumped off again, then back on with a click and a rush of wind on the microphone.

"—never finished the U-boat story. Did Papa find the sub?"

"I love that U-boat story," the captain said, laughing.

"Did Ernest—and you, of course—did you find the sub?" the professor asked.

"Not exactly," Dad answered, "Here's what happened."

NINETEEN

THERE'S NO DARK in the world like night on the Gulf Stream, especially around Bimini, I don't know why. It's like black velvet, you can almost feel the dark on your skin. Of course, I won't say there was no light, because trailing behind the *Pilar* was this eerie glowing road. That time of year, tiny floating plankton comes to the surface. The phosphorescent light from the plankton is a natural warning system. You can see anything that pushes through the water.

I think Papa half expected we would find a similar bright trail churned up in the wake of that U-boat. But we were too far behind. Still, they were damaged, and we were making good speed, a steady eight knots. Add to that the Gulf Stream's northbound drift of five knots and you can see why we were sure we could catch our Krauts.

A few more hours passed when suddenly Winston came charging up from the forward cabin. "I've got it, I've got it!" he yelled. "There's a freighter off Key West just reported seeing a U-boat on the surface. She's cruising north."

"Any distress signal?" Papa asked.

"No. They just gave her location, speed, and direction."

"Since she didn't fire on that freighter, her torpedo tubes might be damaged from ramming the reef," I suggested.

"That could be," Papa agreed, "or she's so badly hurt she's just running for home."

"How soon till we catch her?" I asked.

"At our current speed, we should find her off Miami about sunrise," Winston figured.

That was only three hours away, so no one slept. Everyone was running on pure adrenaline. Patche and Julius checked and rechecked our weapons. Winston was glued to the radio, Papa and I scanned the ocean. When the first rays of morning were pinking up the sky, we were twelve miles off Miami's coast. This was the international shipping lanes, so I don't know why it surprised me when we saw it, but it did.

Captain Fuentes spotted it first. A hundred yards off our

starboard bow there was a color change. The rich blue of the Gulf Stream held a bright rainbow of oil. Then, as we closed in, you could see the heavier black under the water. We had entered a debris slick. A couple of life jackets and a few pieces of wood floated in the oil pool. From the spread, Winston guessed it had been a boat about the size of the *Pilar.* We fished out a couple of small pieces—all that was left of what we soon figured out had been a pretty nice yacht.

The lack of big debris probably meant it hadn't been a torpedo that sank them. An explosion breaks a boat into thousands of small, floating pieces—chunks of wood, pieces of furniture, teak rails and paneling, even groceries. We saw nothing like that. More than likely, the U-boat happened on the yacht and just sliced her in half. That would have meant that there were only two large pieces, and they must have gone down almost instantly. The boat's crew probably never even saw what had hit them.

It bothered the hell out of us. I don't know why the U-boat felt they had to do that. Maybe they were afraid the yacht would give away their position. Maybe they were frazzled from the strain of a long patrol and a wounded boat. Maybe they were just sick, sadistic bastards. Whatever the reason, they'd done it, and it didn't much matter why. Especially to the people who'd gone down with that yacht.

It was a hard dose of reality. That yacht might just as easily have been us. Papa set up a search pattern, but after three hours we had failed to find any bodies. "Bloody damned sharks," Winston cursed, "didn't even leave enough for a funeral."

The time we spent searching put us far enough behind that Papa figured we would never catch up with the U-boat. Personally, I felt damned lucky to have missed the big show-down. But Papa was heartsick. The U-boat was like a wounded lion—he wanted to finish it off, make a clean kill of a dangerous beast. But it was not in the cards.

Whatever the case, Papa chose not to pursue the sub any further. Ahab was letting his whale go, and I think we were all grateful. Papa suggested we head over to Bimini. So we turned east again and trolled some lines—and damned if we didn't pick up two record tunas.

TWENTY

THERE WAS a slight pause on the tape, filled only with the heavy hum of the diesels and the sounds of splashing water.

"Wonderful story, Les," the professor said. "You really should publish some of these tales."

"Then what would you do for tenure?" Dad teased.

A long pause. I heard the wind and the splashing of water and the steady thrum of the big engines. Then Dad said, "Look out there. Days like this you can spit and send the ripples to Cuba."

"Is this normal?" the professor asked.

"Only before really big storms," the captain said.

"Oh . . . ah, how long until we get to Bimini?"

"Maybe a half-hour, not much more," Dad told him.

"Tell me," the professor said after a moment, "did your brother ever give you any advice on writing?"

"He told me to do something else," my father said. "Then when he saw I wasn't going to, he made me understand that I'd picked a tough road, and having him for a brother would make it a hell of a lot tougher."

"Nothing about 'Write what you know'?"

"Oh, hell, man. Papa knew I didn't need that explained. What are you driving at?"

"Nothing, Les. It's just that your stories are truly about some remarkable things."

" 'Truly,' Professor. You seem preoccupied by that idea."

"Ah, well," the professor said cautiously. "It is rather important in my line of work, you know."

"No, I didn't know that," my father said with a small laugh. "But it's important to me, too. Tell me, how do you know when something is true, Doctor?"

"Well, actually, I just try to use my best judgment and, you know, find other sources to confirm it."

"Seems to me that leaves a few big holes. What do you do about something unique?"

"Like your stories?" the professor said nervously.

"You asked me if my brother ever gave me any advice

about writing," my father interrupted, and there was a short pause in which I heard a gull shriek in the distance. "Papa told me once, 'Never hesitate to call a spade a dirty unprintable shovel.' And it's okay to level on good guys also, but more gently. Nothing is worth a damn, except the truth as you know it, feel it, and create it in fiction. He used to say, 'Nobody in England ever sued me over *The Sun Also Rises.*' Yet the characters in it had very real origins and everybody knew it. Some of them went around pleasuring themselves with the identification. So slip it to them, every one. A good story is at its best when the line between truth and fiction remains ambiguous."

"Bimini, gentlemen," the captain called.

"Ahhh—damn, what a beautiful sight."

"Les, can you suggest where I might stay?" the professor asked with a touch of *Please don't leave me.*

"Compleat Angler is nice. You'll like the historical side. Ossie Brown owns it. He's a good man."

"Where are you staying?"

"Oh, I have the use of a friend's houseboat down at Learner docks. It's right past the shark pens. Watch out, there are still sharks in them."

I TURNED OFF THE TAPE, remembering the red houseboat in Bimini. "Miss Isabel's," I said, and my daughter and husband looked up at me. "Miss Isabel owned that houseboat. A nice lady."

"Did you stay there, too, Mom?" Bear wanted to know.

"Many times," I said. "I think I saw a picture of it in one of the boxes. Let me go look."

I went back to the closet under the stairs and pulled out two boxes, fumbling through a remarkable assortment of junk before I found the right one. I dusted off my hands and brought the box into my daughter's room. "This is mostly Bimini stuff."

"Mom, look—you're so young," Bear said, fishing out a picture of me as a teenager walking down King's Highway. It was a fancy name for a dirt road that ran the length of North Bimini. A native junkanew parade danced behind me in the photo with whistles blowing, metal drums playing, and two trumpets that, I remembered, worried more about rhythm than melody. "God, I miss that place. So many wonderful memories." I pulled out a black-and-white shot of the houseboat. "Here it is. I heard it sank in one of the hurricanes in the late eighties. Man, wouldn't it be fun to see how the island has changed?"

"Let's go," Jeff offered. "It's a three-hour drive to Miami and a thirty-minute flight to Bimini."

"Yeah, right," I said, looking around at all of Dad's papers, and remembering that I still had Mom's stuff to sort through. "I'm up to my eyeballs in paperwork. I still have to take care of Mom's estate. And Bear's got school."

"Okay, but don't say I didn't offer," Jeff answered. "How about if we at least finish listening to the tape?"

"Deal," I said.

I pushed the Play button. We heard the rattle of someone fumbling with the microphone, and then the professor's voice. "—thought of just a few questions, I wonder if—"

"Oh, for Christ's sake," I heard my father say. "You're in Bimini, man. Can't you just enjoy a great day on the prettiest island in the world?" And I could picture Dad on the dusty two-lane road, carrying his matching luggage—two brown paper grocery bags that held his trusty Polaroid camera and hundreds of copies of the *Bimini Out-Island News*. Dad always wore khaki pants, a Cuban guayabera shirt, dark-blue sneakers, and a wide-brimmed Bahamian straw hat. It was his Bimini uniform.

"Well, yes," the professor said. "It is a lovely day."

"Open up your eyes, man. Look around. Hey—do you smell that? Go ahead, take a sniff."

"Um—" the professor said. Then we heard a cautious little *sniff sniff,* followed by, "Oh, my," and a huge long *snufffft.* "What a wonderful aroma! What is that?"

"They're baking a fresh batch of Bimini bread. Nothing sweeter in the world." The sound of reggae music blared from a passing car and a voice called, "Hey, mon!" Then came the sound of a motor scooter. Its tinny little horn went bleep-bleep, and a friendly Bahamian called, "Hey, mon, how's my Uncle Les?"

"Great, Noble," Dad cheered. I could picture him raising

his straw hat, wiggling his eyebrows. Bimini was an island of characters and Dad was the reigning king.

"Is there anyone on the island you don't know?" the professor asked.

"Only the tourists," Dad answered, laughing. The tape picked up more street sounds and you could hear sea gulls in the harbor fighting over the discarded bait from the returning fishing boats, and their shrieking mixed with the calls of the backyard roosters. "Isn't this a great place?"

"Lovely. Les, I was wondering—"

"Wonder over this way. I have work to do."

"Oh, hey, look at the size of that fish." I heard the sound of their feet on planking, and I knew where they must be. I closed my eyes and saw the blue hoist down at Bimini's Big Game Club. I pictured a huge marlin hanging on the steel hook, motionless and stiffening in death, with a sheet of paper stuck to its side declaring its weight in waterproof ink. How many hundreds of marlin had I seen hoisted there? How many pictures had Dad taken of arrogant rich men and beautiful dead fish?

If I had any problem with Bimini, it was the way the cocky rich routinely killed beautiful fish for no reason other than a photograph. No one ever ate the marlins. Even the islanders had grown accustomed to this waste. Fight a big fish for hours, club it to death, and then haul it in to be weighed and thrown to the crabs. It wasn't right.

"It's a good-sized blue," Dad was saying on the tape.

"Four-fifty, maybe five hundred pounds. Come on, let's find the fishing marvel who caught it."

There were sounds of footsteps crossing the dock. I knew Dad's routine. On a typical weekend he would climb aboard twenty to thirty sportfishing boats, take photos of the men and their big fish, and write his news copy. Maybe he'd sell a few subscriptions, bill the locals for advertising, and visit with friends. For Dad, Bimini was fun, even when he was working.

"Les, I was hoping we might talk some more."

"What about, Maestro?" Dad chuckled. "I have no more hunting stories."

"Yes, but—well, it occurred to me you that must have some terrific fishing tales."

"Oh, balls—haven't you bled me dry? Watch where you're going."

"Well, here's what I was thinking—"

"I said watch out, you're— *Awwwwwhhhh!*" There was the sound of feet stumbling on a wooden dock, followed by a heavy thud. "Oh, sweet Jesus—"

"My God, that's a big hook," the professor whispered. "Look at the blood—!"

"That, sir—is a gaff," Dad said through gritted teeth. "The blood is caused by the fact that the gaff has entered my foot."

"Oh my God," the professor said in a worried tone. It was the first note of authentic emotion I had heard from him. "Oh, Jesus."

"Calm down, man. I'm the one hurting. You just have to pull the son of a bitch out."

A Jimmy Buffett song suddenly got loud, and a voice called out, "What's going on?"

"We need a doctor," the professor answered. I could hear panic in his voice.

"Hey, is that my gaff?" the new voice asked, coming closer until the man sounded like he was standing over Dad and the professor.

"Yes," Dad grunted, "but it's my foot."

"Wow, that's ugly."

"Christ love a duck—just get the goddamned gaff out of my foot."

"I don't want to hurt you," the professor said with a tremble in his voice.

"Grow some balls, man. It's hurting me *now*."

"What do I do? It's gone clear through the sneaker."

"Very carefully," Dad whispered, "pull the hook straight out. Don't take off the shoe—it comes out—as it went in."

"Yes, but—"

"Do it!"

There was a clattering sound I thought must be the tape recorder hitting the dock, and the recording was muffled for a moment. Then I heard Dad saying, "Steady, now. Just pull her right on through." We heard him gasp a few times, and, "Ahhh, fffffuuuuucccccck."

Bear jumped up startled. "Mom—!"

I waved her back down. "Shh!" I said, leaning forward to hear. The professor was gasping. "I got it," he said at last. "I did it." There was a small note of surprise and triumph in his voice.

"Thank you," Dad said softly.

"You want some ice?" the new voice asked.

"No, bandages," Dad answered.

"Man, that's a lot of blood," the voice added.

"Top quality, too," my father said. "I'd like to keep the rest, if I can."

"Please get some bandages," the professor prodded. You could hear more people walking down the dock, a small crowd forming and whispering, "What happened?" "Wow, looks bad." "Hey, we got blood in the water. Bobbie, get me my spinner."

Dad said softly, "Some days it's tough to be a member of the human race."

More people were walking down the dock, then over the crowd noise I heard the sound of a motor scooter and the beep, beep, beep of its horn. "Uncle Les, you no look so good."

"Thanks, Ossie. Any chance you have a doctor staying in the house?"

"I'll find you one. Come on friends, help Mr. Hemingway. One, two, three lift. Okay—"

Even without Dad saying the man's name, I would have recognized the voice. It was Ossie Brown, a sweet-faced Bahamian who owned the Compleat Angler Hotel.

I was glad Dad was going to Ossie's hotel. I had not known this was where he had been taken. But I remembered that the gaffing incident was what led Dad to see the doctors in Miami who told him he had diabetes.

It suddenly occurred to me what I was listening to. This was no longer a collection of interesting stories and an annoying professor. The tape had just captured the turning point in my family's history. I felt overwhelmed. Here was my Dad sounding so happy, so incredibly alive—and he had no idea that this was the beginning of the end of his life. From this dock in Bimini it was now a short, straight road to hospitals and doctors and operations and, finally, to the cold tile floor inside the front door of our house.

The confused sound of music, a crowd, ice tinkling in glasses came on the tape. *They must be at Ossie's place,* I thought. And sure enough, right away I heard Ossie's voice. "Here, Les. Drink it down. Drink it down, mon."

"Aaahhh. Christ, that's good," I heard my father say.

"What can I do to help?" the professor asked quietly.

A new voice answered. "Keep him talking, it will keep his mind off my needlework." Ossie had found a doctor.

"Well, Les—how about a fishing story?" the professor said.

"Go ahead, Les," the doctor urged him. "If you start talking, you may not notice if I make a few mistakes."

"Hell of a bedside manner, Doc. Try not to sew my foot to the table."

"No promises," the doctor answered, and chuckled.

"All right, Doc—keep the drinks coming."

The professor butted in with the sound of ice rattling in a glass. "Here, Les. Fresh drink."

"Ahhh, bless you."

"So, how about that fishing story, Les?"

I heard Dad take another long drink. Finally he said, "All right, Doc. Hell, the way this foot is already throbbing, I won't sleep much tonight. I might as well talk." He took one more sip. "Okay. The great barracuda—this is a fish that runs a good eight feet and can make short, fast runs at close to forty miles an hour. I've seen them hit a tuna that was as thick as your thigh, chop it right in half. It's so fast, your eye can't follow the action."

"Hear, hear," someone said in the background, followed by the sounds of two or three people laughing.

"Thank you, Nobles. And I have seen the 'cuda strike— Christ, that hurts—!"

"Sorry. Almost done," the doctor said.

"I've seen the 'cuda up close, much closer than I would like. It was the summer of 1941. I was off the western end of Cuba with Papa and his wife, Martha. We had gone for a day's sail, but I had missed one of the local markers and run hard aground.

"We were just waiting for the tide to float us again. And so, trying to make best use of the time and shallow location, I was over the side, scraping the barnacles off the bottom. We had tied the boat to the mangroves at the edge of the channel. While I worked, Papa and Martha sat and read.

"I had no reason to think my life was in danger. A school of small jacks came into the inlet. The first I knew they had been followed was when a fistful of jacks frantically broke water. Their jumps sounded like a hard rain smacking the water. In a single movement, the school scattered to our side of the inlet.

"The jacks were now all around me in the shallows, sprinting to get away from the big slashing fish giving chase. I was in this crystal-clear water, staring at the silver streaks weaving between my bare feet, when I heard Papa yell, 'Look out.' He'd seen the torpedo-shaped barracuda heading right for my leg. Before I could respond the 'cuda struck the scraper in my hand with a flash of teeth."

"Oh God, Les, stop. The tape is running out," the professor interrupted. "Please wait, I have another cassette in my room. Please. I'll just run upstairs and—"

There was a hard click and the tape ended.

"WAIT A MINUTE." I turned and looked at my husband, and then at my daughter. "What just happened?"

"It's over," Jeff said. "That's the end of the tape."

"What about the second tape he went to get?" Bear asked.

"I don't have it," I said. "This is all Mom gave me."

"But I want to hear what happens," Bear said.

"Me too. Damn. There are so many unanswered questions."

"Write them out," Jeff said.

I grabbed a piece of paper. "Okay." I thought for a moment. "Who's the professor? How did Mom get this tape?"

"Where's the second tape?" Bear added.

"Are the stories even partly true?" Jeff threw in.

I scribbled everything down, thinking about all I had just heard. The tape had whipped me through an emotional amusement park; up one minute and way down the next. I could not shake all the images of my father that came from listening to these stories. And even though making the list was just a way to stop thinking about it for a few minutes, I knew I would keep coming back to wondering until I knew. "There are plenty of questions," I said, finally looking up at Jeff. "But where do we go for answers?"

"Bimini," Bear said, and we both turned to look at her.

TWENTY-ONE

EVERY GOOD PLAN of action takes time. I would love to tell you that immediately after hearing Daddy's tape, my family and I ran right to all the answers, but in truth, it wasn't like that.

Over the next six weeks I finished working through my mom's estate papers. No one tells you how much paperwork there is in dying, but it far outweighs the documentation for being born. I had to see lawyers, accountants, and bankers, and then plan the joint interment of Mom's and Dad's ashes.

During this time, I also spent at least an hour a day transcribing the professor's tape. It seemed to take forever, especially when the Barney tape player died. I also began to realize the real limitations I faced as a dyslexic typist. But finally the tape was transcribed.

In this same six-week period Jeff had the tough and dusty job of going through the boxes and sorting Dad's papers. By the time he was done organizing the stories and separating out those that were incomplete, we were left with fifty-two complete story manuscripts. Some of them were on hunting, war, or fishing. Others described wild locations for camping, exploring, and treasure-hunting.

We found that many of the stories from the professor's tape did correspond with stories Dad had written—with one glaring exception. Dad had not included Papa's character in any of his written stories. His insights on Ernest as a brother, a man, and a writer had been given solely for the professor's benefit. As I knew well, my father did not talk about Ernest unless directly asked—and often not even then. So why had he chosen to enlighten the professor, and why through the use of these tales?

As for the hunts themselves, the amount of detail began to convince me that my father had actually lived many of these wild adventures. But even those he had not actually experienced, he had so thoroughly researched that it was hard to tell fact from fiction. After talking to relatives and friends, and looking through passport papers, we do believe Dad traveled in Europe, Africa, Central and South America, throughout the

Caribbean, and of course, in the United States. We didn't find any proof that my father ever went to China, and aside from the tiger's claw I saw as a child, I have no evidence that he was ever in India.

That was our basic evidence. And of course it wasn't enough. We had just as many questions as ever. Most of our questions about this tape, including how and why it came back to my mother, could have been answered by a half-hour chat with the professor. We did discover transcripts of interviews Dad did with some of the Hemingway scholars, including several very well-known biographers: Carlos Baker, author of *Hemingway, A Life Story;* Denis Brian, *The True Gen;* and Bernice Curt, *The Hemingway Women.* But unlike what he did with the professor on my tape, Dad did not present his responses to these questions in story form. Perhaps the interviewers did not annoy him enough—or more likely, their interviews came after the gaffing incident when my father had given up drinking.

But we couldn't know for sure. And except for the professor, the only folks who could have told us anything were dead: Dad, Charlie Willeford, and my mom.

Jeff tried to locate the professor through the Internet. He looked for scholarly papers regarding Papa's more unusual hunts and, failing that, he searched for any magazine articles on the same subject. He could find nothing that wasn't already documented in conventional sources. More out of whimsy than from any real hopes of a result, Jeff even did a search for any variations of the name Leech—including Leach, Leache, Lietsch, and Liech. And although he found quite a few doctors with some variation of the name, none of them was an English professor.

We were sitting at dinner discussing this one evening when T. L. Bear frowned and said, "Well, whoever he was—wouldn't he have the second tape? Then we could prove it."

"That's great. Kind of like the glass slipper." Jeff chuckled. "If someone comes forward saying they're Professor Leech—we have a way to check it."

"Unless of course, we already have it," I countered. "You did go through all of Dad's boxes when you got his stories together, right?"

"No. I just pulled out papers, manuscript pages, and letters. A second tape could be in there, I guess. There was a lot of stuff I didn't get into."

"I know what we're doing," Bear sang, "after dinner."

We stayed up late that night and began anew the next morning. After six hours, we had gotten through only six more boxes. You cannot believe how hard it is to sift through your father's photos and keepsakes and not find yourself lost in memories. There were letters regarding New Atlantis, NA stamps sheets, clay Mayan fertility dolls. We found clippings from Grandmother Grace's art showings, a ton of family photos and reference material from Dad's biography, *My Brother, Ernest Hemingway,* and stacks of copies of Dad's *Bimini Out-Island News.*

But T. L. Bear made the big discovery at the bottom of box number six. Not the second tape, but it was almost as good.

"What's this, Mom?" Bear asked, holding up a green velvet pouch. I could see the flaking gold letters on one side that read "Bimini Big Game Club."

"Huh—Big Game Club. That's a nice hotel. What's in it?"

"Wasn't that the dock where your dad hurt his foot?" Jeff asked.

"Yeah, it was—here, let me help you," I offered as Bear fumbled with the bag's strings.

"I can do it myself," she said, and eventually undid the knot and dumped some of the contents onto the living room rug.

The first thing to hit the ground was a gnarled, dried-out thing that I identified only after a moment of shock so complete I forgot to breathe.

It had to be a monkey's finger.

Bear shook the remaining contents of the pouch onto the carpet. We saw the dull casing of a .22, a crocodile tooth, an ostrich spur, large scales from a reptile of some kind—a cobra?—then a few other animal parts I wasn't sure of—and a tiger's claw.

Jeff picked up the tiger's claw and held it up to the light.

"Wow. Recognize this? You said your dad had a tiger's claw in his wallet when you were a kid."

I took the claw from Jeff and looked at it. "Dad's tiger's claw." After a moment I answered, "This is really it." I looked down at the rest of the strange dried-out animal charms. "My God."

"I told you it was true!" Bear said, pointing the monkey's finger at me accusingly.

"It can't be," I said, still in shock.

"Why not?" Jeff asked. The idea seemed so far-fetched moments ago, but after this finding, I was no longer sure what to think.

"Oh, man, oh God." I flopped back against the couch and stared blankly at the ceiling. "This is crazy."

"What's wrong, Mom?" Bear asked.

"This," I said, holding up the tiger's claw.

"Okay, fine. Beat yourself up," Jeff said, "They're just dried animal parts—feed them to the dog."

I picked up the monkey's finger and saw how the hairs were dropping off like on an old rabbit's foot. "It just can't be."

Jeff put his arm around my shoulder. "When I was doing the research, I discovered a story filed by William Walton, a correspondent from *Time* magazine, who reported that Papa himself once led on some visiting academics with fantastic tall tales. Hell—it's probably a family tradition. For all we know this stuff is nothing more than props for the stories."

I shook my head, still feeling numb. "No. Too weird. I never, ever saw my father lie about his life or his brother's. Why make it up when they lived it?"

"So now you think the stories are true?" Bear asked.

"I didn't say that."

"Well, but—why does it matter, anyway?" Bear asked. "I like the stories. I don't care if they're true. I just wish there were more stories. I want to know what happens when they go fishing for Mr. 'Cuda."

I laughed. "You're right. It doesn't matter. But—I wouldn't mind knowing what really happened. It's our family history, after all."

"I've been thinking about that." Jeff began. "How about if we go to Bimini this weekend? See if we can find anybody who was there the day your dad got hurt?"

"After all these years?"

He smiled. "Come on, somebody is bound to remember. How often does a Hemingway get gaffed?"

CHALKS AIRLINE STILL FLIES out of Watson Island on Miami Beach. And aside from the $190 round-trip tickets—I remembered them as $39—much of the seaplane service to Bimini was still the same. It was the same old sixteen-seater prop plane, the engines as loud as ever. After boarding, you rolled down the ramp into Biscayne Bay. For anyone who ever had a nightmare about driving a car into a lake, this can be disturbing. But seaplanes do float, and with a roar of engines, we took off down Government Cut. Below us the cars driving along MacArthur Causeway magically turned into Matchbox toys. The crowds along South Beach looked like so many ants.

It's fair to say that Miami had changed more than Bimini in the time I'd been away. Of course, both went through Hurricane Andrew. But the folks in Bimini didn't get a chance to rip off the insurance companies for billions of dollars and rebuild, redesign, and remove all the landmarks I had grown up with. In fact, much of the island looks exactly the same. Chalks still pulls up at the south end of North Bimini. The majority of islanders still walk along the paved but sandy King's Highway. About the only addition to the island I could see were golf carts—lots of them.

We cleared customs and flagged down one of the island's three working taxis. It was a stripped-out Chevy van. For twenty dollars, the driver told us, he could take us anywhere on the island. This could be all the way to the far end, Alice Town, three miles away, or just around the corner. Either way, it was twenty bucks. Since I couldn't remember how far the Compleat Angler Hotel was from the airport, we decided to walk. As it turned out, two blocks later, that was a good call.

I was holding Pookie, while Jeff and Bear took care of our bags. Bear couldn't take her eyes off the harbor.

"What is it?" I asked.

"It's just so clear. I didn't know water could be so clear."

"Yeah," I said, grinning. "Wait till you see the beach on the other side."

We passed a half-dozen small shops. They weren't fancy boutiques in the Key West sense, though some did sell clothes. These were truly mom-and-pop stores, selling day-to-day items: food, soap, toothpaste. I stopped in one with a sign in the window—Bimini Bread. The loaf was two bucks, and I paid it gladly. If it was half as good as I remembered, I would have paid that per slice.

"I'll carry it for you, Mommy," Bear said, sniffing greedily at the package.

"Not on your life."

We continued on past the old customs building. I was pleased that it was still there, even though it was still a shell. It had burned one night in the early seventies. Bimini customs had stumbled on a disabled Jamaican freighter and pulled in a record haul of marijuana. And soon after they had loaded it into the customs building, a fire had broken out. Dad had always doubted that the evidence had really burned up so conveniently. It struck him as a little suspicious when the island's only fire station was right next door.

One of the nicest things about Bimini is that the coconut trees are healthy; they haven't suffered from lethal yellowing like those in Florida. The way the branches swayed in the wind, the sound of the light tapping of their leaves, the smell of the Bimini Bread in my hand—it was all reassuring. I was filled with a sense that I had finally come home, and aside from having my daughters at my side, instead of being the daughter at my father's side, Bimini was the same. I took a deep breath and savored the sweet smell of diesel mixed with old fish rot.

"Look, Bear." I pointed at the huge piles of pink conch shells in the shallows. "Conchs. Aren't they pretty?"

"Can I have one?" Bear asked.

"Not if it stinks like that," Jeff told her.

We hurried on and came to a one-story white building. "Miss Opal's. Hey, this was where Daddy used to take us to eat. The food was always great—and—"

"Let me guess," Jeff interrupted, "always cheap."

"You got it." I laughed and peeked in. There were a few locals watching TV and an American couple drinking coffee. There were still a half-dozen tables with plastic tablecloths and fresh hibiscus flowers.

"Oh, man," I said. "It's just like it was."

"Good, then we can have lunch here," Jeff said.

Just past Miss Opal's was the Compleat Angler Hotel. Of all the hotels on the island, I had always liked Ossie's best. It was not a stamped-from-a-mold franchise, and it could not have existed anywhere but Bimini. It had real character. Not because the walls were loaded with photos of Ernest and framed pages from *Islands in the Stream*. The hotel's character came from the warm feeling you got when you went inside, and from the design of the building. The natural dark wood, the fine detail in the colonial style—it was a beautiful piece of history, and I had always felt at home there.

We entered the yard through a stone fence shaped like a boat frame, and walked through a small courtyard filled with pink and red hibiscus and up to the old wooden porch. "The last time I sat here—I was with Dad and Dr. Engle. We ate fresh conch with a little lime juice. Tastes like lobster gum."

"Sounds great, Mom," Bear said, rolling her eyes. "I'll be sure to try that."

We stepped inside the dark lobby. The wood paneling always made this place seem darker. I waited a moment for my eyes to adjust. Bear had no problem with the light change and immediately found the ring-toss game that hung from the wall.

"Hi," I said to the Bahamian at the registration desk. He was too young to be Ossie, but I thought he might be related. "I made reservations. My name is Hilary Hemingway."

"Let me see." He ran his pencil down the day book. "Ahh, here you are. Two adults, one child, and a baby, non-smoking."

"That's us." He made no apparent connection to my name, or to the fact that Papa pictures were plastered all over their wall. Perhaps they had Hemingways staying here all the time— a dime a dozen. I didn't ask. In a way, it was a relief. We took the room key and went upstairs.

It was a nice clean wood-paneled room, with a queen-size bed, a crib, and a small rollaway in the corner for Bear. I didn't really want to mess with unpacking as much as I wanted to show my daughter and husband the island, so we did a quick change of clothing and headed back down to the street. I brought along the velvet bag, determined to find answers.

About a block north, we found the Bimini Big Game Club. We went in and I walked up to the front desk, and pulled the old green bag from my purse.

"I know this is going to sound a little strange, but I was hoping that you could help us."

"Yes, ma'am. I hope so, too," the manager said.

"I found this bag in my father's things. Can you tell us what it's used for or—I don't know—what might have been in it?"

"Smooth," Jeff whispered close to my ear. "Ask him if they run a special on monkey fingers."

The Bahamian smiled. "We used to give those out for people to put jewelry or keepsakes in, then we put them in our office safe. But not any more." The man handed the bag back. "Anything else, ma'am?"

"No." I shook my head, disappointed. "Um, thank you." He smiled, and we walked back through the lobby toward the pool and deck in the courtyard. Beyond the retaining wall, I saw a vacant lot. "That's where the Learner Lab used to be. The shark pens and docks are gone—I guess some things do change."

"It was just the bag, honey," Jeff said. "What about that guy who helped your dad? The guy who owned the hotel."

"Ossie Brown." I smiled, remembering his sweet voice and warm personality.

"That's the one," Jeff answered. "Let's find Ossie."

"What about lunch?" Bear asked. Pookie began to squirm in my arms and I could feel she needed a diaper change. "Okay," I said. "Let's get back to the hotel." Having kids is like going on permanent safari. Just when you're sure you have packed everything, you find you still have to return to base camp for supplies and ammunition.

At our room at the Compleat Angler, Jeff and I got the kids taken care of, and after a round of diapers and juice boxes I went down to the front desk and found the same young man who had checked us in. "Excuse me," I said, waiting for eye contact. "I'm trying to find Mr. Ossie Brown?"

"Ossie?"

"Yes, he was the owner of this hotel. My father knew him quite well."

"I'm sorry."

"Sorry for what?"

"About two years ago, Mr. Ossie have an accident. A mon he don't even know come at him with a big pipe wrench. He smack poor Ossie in the head."

"My God, is he okay?"

"Okay? No, what you thinkin'? Ossie dead."

"Oh, God. I'm so sorry." I turned and walked away. I didn't know what to say. I found Jeff and Pookie watching Bear in the far room as she threw a brass ring tied to the end of a long string at a nail hung on the wall.

"So are we going to talk to Ossie?" Jeff asked, handing Pookie to me to take his turn at the ring toss.

"Not unless we have a psychic." I watched the ring touch the nail, then drop away.

"Close, but no cigar," Bear said.

"Exactly." It took me a moment before I realized that she was commenting on the ring-toss game. "If there are any answers in Bimini, I don't see how we're ever going to find them."

Jeff looked at me hard, and I guess he saw my disappointment. "Come on. Let's walk," he said.

We headed back down to Miss Opal's and ate cracked conch. Or Jeff and I did; Bear was quite pleased with a PB&J on Bimini bread. Pookie had a jar of Gerber oatmeal. Maybe the food just settled my blood sugar, but sitting with my family and eating the good, simple food cheered me up. What the hell, I had finally come back to Bimini with my family, and it was still the place I remembered. I reached across the table for Jeff's hand. He took it and waggled his eyebrows at me.

"Let's put the quest on hold for a while," he said. "There's still lots to do here."

I smiled. "You're right. And I know just where to start," I said. I got the kids cleaned up while he paid the bill, and we strolled down to Weaches dock and set up a boat rental for the next morning.

We spent the rest of the day walking through the island gift shops. I picked up a straw hat and tried it on. "What do you think?"

"Your dad would be proud," Jeff said.

"Let's all get them." Bear was trying on a lovely green braided hat with an ornamental bird dangling from the side. She found another just like it and put it on Pookie's head. Pookie laughed and tried to grab the bouncing birdie, but it was too fast for her.

We strolled slowly through the town and finally found the stairs that led down to the beach on the north side. The sand was as white as sugar. The water was cooler than I remembered, but then I had spent mostly summers in Bimini, and never a February.

Jeff unpacked a couple of beers for us, an orange soda for Bear, and a juice bottle for Pookie. We had sausage and bread for dinner. We swam and played until sunset and then watched the glorious colors fill the sky. Pink and orange diamonds danced on the surface of the ocean. It was too beautiful and too full of good memories for me to stay unhappy. I drank my beer and smiled.

"Better?" Jeff asked.

"I'm glad we came," I said. "If that tape has done nothing else, at least it's given me Bimini back."

"Uh-huh," Jeff said. "This place is perfect."

"Hey, hey, hey," Bear said, slapping her leg. "I'm getting bitten by something."

"Oh, the no-see-ums. Let's get out of here." A moment later, Pookie began to cry from bites. I picked her up and wrapped her in a towel. "It's okay, Pook. Even paradise has a bug or two."

"Last one back is a rotten conch," Jeff teased. He already had on his shoes and he quickly gathered most of our things. Bear and I followed as fast as we could. We were halfway down the hill when we heard the music blasting from the Compleat Angler.

"Is that our hotel?" Bear asked.

"Oh God—the nightly band."

"You knew about this?" Jeff did not look happy.

"Um—I guess I forgot."

As we entered the boat-shaped gate, the reggae beat was almost deafening. The bushes shook with the throbbing bass and we could hardly move through the courtyard filled with dancing couples.

"How could you forget this?" Bear shouted.

"Selective memory," I yelled back. "Maybe it won't be so bad in our room!"

But it was. With the door closed and damp towels covering the door frame and window, we succeeded in muffling the vocals a little, but the whole building seemed to be moving to the reggae beat. Bear fell asleep with her pillow wrapped around her head. Pookie cried for half an hour more and then fell asleep. Jeff and I stayed awake until two, when the band finally packed up, and then he slept.

I could not sleep.

My body was exhausted, but my mind was racing. Maybe it was just the lateness of the hour, but all my unanswered questions had come creeping back.

Why had Mom given me this tape? What purpose was it supposed to serve? She loved Dad, she loved me. I had no doubts about that at all. So why give me the tape? Was it supposed to bridge the gap left by his suicide? Or was I looking too deep? Maybe there had never been any purpose—she just left the tape to me because she couldn't stand to throw it away.

But what about the stories? She knew I was the family member who continued to write. And she knew how desperately I missed Dad. But the stories—

Whatever the case, the stories were now mine.

And so were the questions that went with them.

THE MORNING SUN ROSE with the sound of sea gulls and roosters' cries. Then, as people began moving about, the air filled with sounds of moped engines and the low rumble of boat diesels from the waterfront. We walked down to Miss Opal's for breakfast and then back to our room to pack for our boat ride. On an impulse I couldn't explain, I tossed in Daddy's tape and the velvet bag with the animal charms. We made it to Weaches dock by eight. There were several skiffs at the dock and an old sportsfishing boat tied up at the end that turned out to be our rental. It was a thirty-year-old Bertram, around twenty-five feet long, still a nice boat in spite of showing its age a bit. We had it for a half-day bare-boat rental. We didn't plan on fishing, so we had no captain, mate, or fishing gear.

Our plan was to pack a lunch and head out for the Three Sisters, three huge coral rocks that sit in only twenty feet of water off North Bimini. I knew the snorkeling was good there. It's one of the few places in the world still teeming with fish life. So we topped off the fuel tanks, loaded in some ice, and headed out.

Jeff ran the boat from the fly bridge, while the girls and I sat on the stern looking at the water. "It's like we're at an aquarium," Bear said. "The water's so clear."

"Coo-ah," Pookie agreed. It was still her favorite word.

"The prettiest water in the world," I told her. "I can't tell you how many times I've jumped in, thinking it was just a few feet deep, and discovered I was in way over my head."

"Three Sisters coming up," Jeff called down to us from the bridge.

"Come on Bear, get your swim stuff together."

Jeff idled the boat as close as he dared to the reef. I threw out the anchor and Jeff came down the ladder and yanked hard to set it. Then we sat for a moment in the quiet, enjoying the sound of the sea lapping the hull.

When you have kids, the quiet never lasts long. Bear came boiling up from below, a dive mask perched on her head. "What are we waiting for?" she demanded.

"You," Jeff answered. "Let's go!"

In the next few moments, both he and Bear had jumped in. I got Pookie into her swimsuit with its built-in float ring. I swam next to her and had to laugh at the face she made when she stuck her tongue out to lick the salt.

My girls, here in Bimini, I thought with quiet satisfaction.

"Mom!" Bear called through her snorkel. She had surfaced closer to the coral head. "You got to see these fish. They're blue and yellow."

"Sure, triggerfish. They don't bite."

I swam closer, towing Pookie, and watched as Jeff wrestled a spiny lobster from its hidey-hole. Bear kicked slowly to follow the living veil of blue and yellow fish working their way around the rocks. Then suddenly she gurgled and swam back to me at full speed. I saw a huge black manta come around the corner, like a great slow bird. Its shiny wings kicked up bottom-sand with each beat. "Manta," I told Bear. "It's all right. It won't hurt you." She turned to look, and I watched her as wonder replaced panic. "Awesome," she said as the manta finally swam off into the distance.

After an hour of swimming, the fins were beginning to

chafe my feet and my mask felt glued to my face. So Pookie and I climbed out and dried off. I was getting her fed, when Jeff and Bear tossed their fins onto the deck and climbed up the dive platform.

I looked over at Jeff and Bear. They sat on the transom, dripping wet and grinning at each other, at me, at the bright sunshine and the beautiful water.

"I'm very glad we came to Bimini," I said.

"Me too," Bear said.

Jeff walked over and gave me a kiss. "It's been a great day," he said. And it had. Even Pookie seemed to agree.

Our time was almost up, but we wanted to make the day last. So Jeff took the long way back to the dock, out into the deep water around the island. And as we moved slowly through the color change and into the deep, I went up onto the flying bridge. Bear was balanced on Jeff's lap, helping him steer the boat.

"It's been a great time," Jeff said. "Even if we didn't find any earth-shattering answers."

"Who says we didn't?" I shifted Pookie in my arms as she fussed. I reached into my shoulder bag for her juice bottle. It was lying on top of the velvet bag with its faded gold letters. I gave Pookie her bottle, then lifted out the pouch and the old cassette tape that had brought us here. "I think a day like this one, being here in Bimini with my family—I think maybe that's the real answer." I looked down from the bridge and out at the slow-moving swells coming in from the ocean. We hadn't found Ossie or anything more about the gaffing incident or the professor, but I realized that I was no longer depressed. "I think we should enjoy Dad's stories for what they are—stories. Nothing more, nothing less."

"That's the way I like them," Bear said.

Jeff leaned over and kissed the top of my head. "If you're happy, I'm happy."

I looked at the tape and pouch. "We don't need this stuff," I said. "The tape was meant to remind me of my father's love of life and adventure. It did that. If we place more value on the tape, or these animal trophies, we've made the same mistake the professor did."

I looked out at the deep clean water and felt the rightness of what I had just said. Hanging onto the tape, scurrying around to prove whether it was true or not true—that was just undermining the real value of the tape and the reason I was now sure my mother had left it for me.

And so I steadied Pookie on my hip, cocked back my arm, and flung the bag and the tape far out over the transom and into the deep, blue Bimini water.

"Hey!" Jeff called out, and Bear lunged up to her feet, staring in horror, but it was too late. I was a pretty good softball player and this was a good throw. The tape and the velvet bag of charms landed with a splash about thirty yards back. They swirled in the white water of our wake and then went under.

"Why did you do that?" Bear demanded. More puzzled than angry, like it was the last thing she had expected me to do. I put an arm around my older daughter. "Remember your grandfather saying, 'Truth is a strange thing, kid'? Well, I think I just figured it out."

"But those things were the only proof we had," Bear protested.

I just shook my head. "No. Like Kreskin says: If you believe, no proof is necessary, and if you don't, no proof is possible. And that's the real truth. Dad's stories are all that's important. Not finding the professor, the second tape, or anything else. The stories are for you, for me, for everyone, to know my dad as he really was, a man who had the courage to love life. That's why Mom gave the tape to me."

Jeff looked at me for a long moment. Then he shook his head, reached down to open our beach bag, and pulled out a bottle of wine. "Since this is our last day here in Paradise, I thought I'd surprise you. Of course," he said, nodding toward where I had thrown the tape and the velvet bag, "you got me first."

He uncorked the bottle and held it up. "Isn't this a great day?" he said, a pretty fair imitation of the way my father had said it on the tape. Then he handed the bottle to me. "Go ahead. Make a little toast."

I held the bottle in my hand. It was still slightly cool, and a drop of condensation ran down the side and onto my foot. It really had been a great day, I thought. I held up the bottle in salute. "Cheers, Mom, Dad, Uncle Ernest," I said, looking out over the bright blue ocean. "Thanks for everything." I felt the tears start, and because I felt happier than I had in months, I wondered why I was crying. And then I knew.

Here, in the beautiful blue water of Bimini, I was crying for them all, for Dad and for my mother, because at last, after almost fifteen years of holding it in, I finally could. For the first time, I could really mourn my father. And as I realized that, I thought about my mother, too, and why she had left me the battered cassette tape. She had left the tape knowing I would listen to it, and knowing how I would feel when I did. It was Mom's final great gift to me.

She had given me back my father.

Leicester Hemingway in Bimini, 1979

Hubert Humphrey with Les

The Blue Stre...

The Miami Beach estate

Hail to the Chief

TERRITORY OF THE
SOVEREIGN REPUBLIC
OF
NEW ATLANTIS

NORTON MOCKRIDGE

A Littl...

...ESTER HEMINGWAY is t...
...man in the world, I think, wh...
...his country, who built it hims...
...s acting president and only citi...
...o figures to make a fabulous fo...
...d it.

Leicester's
called the
Republic of
lantis, certa...
anything to...
right now.
eight squa...
just three...
above sea...
stuck tog...
bamboo p...
pipes, sta...
cables and...
—but in ...

...ing to Leicester, it's going ...
more than a platinum mine.
To be painfully honest, h...
merely a raft. But it's anch...
and cable to a rock shelf j...
...Caribbean, a ...

50 CENTES *POSTAGE

NEW ATLANTIS * POSTAGE

free world

NEW ATL...

864

20 CENTES

NEW ATL...